T

Praise for The Home Within

There are journeys that take us across borders, and there are journeys that take us deeper within. For me, the practice of empathy — and especially self-empathy — has been that inner path I have relied upon as I lived around the world. I do not see this intentional skill as indulgence, or even as choice, but as survival. To understand ourselves and where we belong is not only essential to our health and longevity, but it is also the only sustainable way to gather the scattered parts of ourselves when life asks us to begin again. And as most professional women in the global economy will tell you, it asks this of us often.

In *The Home Within*, Nina reminds us with such beauty that belonging is not about geography, but about memory, resilience, and the courage to listen to our own inner voice. Her stories echo so many of my own reflections — from the long hours spent learning how to soften toward myself, to the revelation of finally naming truths I had carried silently. And, most importantly, the reminder of how vital it is to honour the connections that sustain, surround, and fulfil us. They are everything.

What Nina has created here is an invitation — to all of us, as women, as mothers, as community leaders — to remember that while our individual stories may differ, the human search for belonging is universal. And when we dare to tell our stories with honesty, as she does here, we discover they become the very connections we need not only to survive, but to thrive. Connections back to each other. And, perhaps most importantly, connections back to ourselves.

And maybe this is what we all need now, more than ever.

Mimi Nicklin, United Kingdom/Malaysia
International Bestselling Author & Empathy Advocate

It is absolutely brilliant! This is truly remarkable... The way you weave together nature, philosophy, human emotions and deep reflection is both profound and beautiful. It truly resonates with me!

Tengku Mazura Tengku Ismit, Malaysia
Chief Compliance Officer

I love the content of your book. It's so relatable... Like you are writing my thoughts.

Zhana Hanizan, Malaysia, Singer

You write so beautifully! I cried a bit in the part about your mama..

Maylene Seah, Singapore/United Kingdom
Award-Winning Brand Strategist

I started Chapter 9 ... and you just killed me with the first words! What a true reality... Amazing work!

Belen Elgueta Leon, Chile/The Netherlands
Video Gaming Expert

Wow! Just great! Your words are beautiful ...

Betsy Lindsey, USA / The Netherlands
Chief Operating Officer

It is sublime, inspiring and I am so touched.

Juliana Nasir, Malaysia/Hong Kong/France
Educator

The Home Within

A Soulful Memoir of Self-Belonging Across Cultures and Change

Nina Aziz Justin

The Resilience Mentor

Copyright

The Home Within: A Soulful Memoir of Self-Belonging Across Cultures & Change

First Edition — Amsterdam, The Netherlands

www.theresiliencementor.com

Disclaimer

This independent publication is not affiliated with any company, organisation, or individual mentioned. All trademarks remain the property of their respective owners.

The content is based on the author's lived experience and personal reflections. Names are used on a first-name basis. Events are remembered to the best of the author's ability and may differ from others' recollections.

Inspired by disciplines like neuroscience, philosophy and psychology, but no formal sources are cited. AI tools supported editing for clarity. The cover was created using Canva Pro under its Content Licence Agreement.

The author is not liable for any errors, omissions, or consequences resulting from the use of this book.

Printed and published by The Resilience Mentor

ISBN: 9789090405803

Formatted with Vellum

To The Explorers, the Braves and The Misfits
— may you always find your way home.

Mama
My first home.
Ayah
The silent current in my veins.
David
My forever harbour.
Camilla & Isabel
My brightest lighthouses, ever guiding me home.

“Jauh berjalan, luas pandangan.”
The farther you journey, the wider your vision.

Contents

Foreword

I first met Nina at boarding school in 1985. Isolated from our families and adjusting from city life to a small town, many of us struggled. Yet it was within those challenges that we discovered a kind of sisterhood in one another — bonds that gave us strength, laughter, and belonging.

As the years unfolded, our journeys carried us far beyond the walls of that school and the borders of Malaysia. We stepped outside our comfort zones to pursue education, careers, and dreams. Though our paths diverged, they converged again in 2021, when I was appointed Ambassador of Malaysia to the Netherlands, where Nina had been living with her family.

There is something profound about meeting someone from your past after decades apart. Time is evident in our faces, our words, our ways — and yet some things never change. Nina is still the active, warm, and determined person I once knew. To witness her growth as a mother, entrepreneur, strategist, public speaker, and now writer has been deeply inspiring. It is a privilege to write this foreword for her.

At its heart, this book is about identity — what shapes it, and how it evolves through the years. For Southeast Asian women especially, identity is layered with expectations handed down to us: to nurture, to provide, to preserve. How do we reconcile these inherited roles with our own ambitions?

As Ambassador, I have carried the duty of representing Malaysia's interests and values abroad. Nina, in her own way, has carried a similar responsibility as a global strategist, often serving as the first encounter people have with Malaysia in her field. She reminds us to ask: can cultural duty and personal ambition coexist, or must one be surrendered for the other?

In 2022, I had the pleasure of visiting the Van Gogh Museum with Nina and our daughters. We admired *The Potato Eaters*, *Sunflowers*, and my personal favourite, *Almond Blossoms*. Yet it was the sketches that struck me most — proof that genius lies not only in talent, but in process and perseverance. So too with identity: it is never a single portrait, but a mosaic, shaped by our experiences, surroundings, and relationships.

I ended my diplomatic service in the Netherlands with Nina welcoming my family into her Amsterdam home. Now she welcomes readers into *The Home Within*. If you are feeling lost in your identity, compelled to step beyond your four walls, or searching for a reflection of your own journey, this book will meet you where you are.

I hope you find inspiration in Nina's journey, as I have.

Her Excellency Dato' Nadzirah Osman,
The Permanent Representative & Ambassador
The United Nations
Geneva, Switzerland

Preface

This book was not written to instruct or impress. It was written to walk beside you. Think of it less as a guide, more as a lantern — something to carry as you wander, question, and remember your own way home.

What you hold is not polished into perfection. In the spirit of *wabi-sabi*, I have let its edges remain a little wild, its lines wander, its rhythm unfold the way real life does: tender, messy, never twice the same.

These pages are not instructions, but invitations. They hold stories of leaving and landing, of grief and grace, of science and spirit, of the slow architecture of becoming.

The book is shaped in three parts — *The Departure, The Becoming, The Return* — each carrying its own note, yet together forming one song. You may read them front to back or as the spirit leads.

Above all, this book is meant to keep you company. To remind you that home is not a single place, but an ongoing return to the self you are always becoming.

Carry what speaks to you. Leave what does not. And let these words be a small light whenever the path ahead feels dim.

— Nina

Prologue

A Journey Without a Map

When people ask me where I'm from, I pause. Not because I don't know — I do. But because "where I'm from" has never fit neatly into one line on a form.

It is a mosaic: migrations and memories, cities I've loved, kitchens where I've wept. It is layered with languages, lined with pivots and dreams. It is not a postcode. It is a feeling.

I carry within me the hospitality of a Malay soul, the tenderness shaped by the tropics, a reverence for soft hearts, for family, for the sacred and ordinary alike. And yet, my story is not only Malaysia's. It is the story of a woman formed by many shores — a heart that belongs to the world as much as to any homeland.

My roots taught me generosity. The world taught me to stretch, to question, to reinvent. I have lived across five countries, built bridges with strangers across dining tables, airports, boardrooms, and mosques. Some of those journeys were carefully mapped.

Others, I followed through a silent ache — the one without a name, calling me outward and inward at once.

This journey has always been full of contradiction and longing. There is the ache of loss. The friction of change. The letting go of certainty. The unexpected birth of something unnamed. And yet, there is also the triumph of authenticity, the wonder of adventure, and the soul's capacity for love — of the world, of life, of self — gently, wholly, everywhere.

What I have come to know is this: leaving home is never just about geography. It is not logistics. It is becoming. It is an emotional shift. A neurological stretch. A spiritual reassembly. It rewires your brain, widens your eyes, and asks your soul to lead before you feel ready. It is thrilling and terrifying. Liberating and lonely. Beautiful and brutal.

This book is not a checklist.

It is not a visa guide or a to-do list in disguise.

It is a companion for the inward journey — the one that begins the moment you whisper: *What if I lived a life beyond what I was handed?*

It is for the ones who have already crossed oceans and still feel unsteady. For the ones standing at the edge, wondering if they are allowed to want more. For the brave. The misfits. The restless hearts. The reluctant wanderers. For those who left to find something. For those who left to lose what no longer fit.

Inside these pages, you will find reflections stitched with neuroscience, with spiritual tools, with stories of grief, humour, and hope. A mix of truth and tenderness. A reminder that you are not alone in your wondering.

Because moving away is never just about finding a new home. It is about finding a new you. Or perhaps — finally coming home to the version of yourself who was always waiting.

So welcome. Let us walk this together — across borders, through seasons, into self.

This is your invitation: to unearth, to unbecome, to rebuild.

To fall in love with the messy flow and sacred architecture of your home within.

— *Nina*

An Offering

"... To self and to all who wander"

Dear Self,

Pause. Place your hand on your heart. Feel what it means to claim your life — not only the pages that shine with kindness and love, but also the tangled ones scribbled with pain, doubt, longing, and all the questions that make you alive.

Remember the child you were: fragile, open, stepping into a world you did not choose, carried by forces older than memory. Remember how you have crossed continents and invisible thresholds within — the borders of identity, belonging, and worth.

It is wild that any of us survive this ride: the heartbreaks, the wild joys, the long nights of loneliness, the unexpected moments of luck that arrive just in time. The hands that helped you, named and unnamed, showed up when you needed them most.

And still, you kept going.

Mistakes, heartbreak, loss, becoming someone new in a world that demanded you rewrite yourself. Yet you kept reaching. You refused to shrink. You lived in the tension between who you were, who you are, and who you might yet be. How rare it is to be this persistent. How silently fierce.

If I could, I would pull you into my arms until every part of you knew: you are safe.

You are allowed.

You belong to yourself completely.

You are already home.

So let this be a pause for gratitude — for every step that carried you here, and every step survived by anyone reading these words. For every fall, and every time you rose again. For the days you questioned everything and still kept going. For the nights you held your own fragile light, even when it barely reached the edge of the room. For the silent forgiveness you offered when no one else could see, and the mercy you learned to give yourself.

I am in awe of your resilience — not the glossy kind, but the deep persistence of carrying on through heartbreak and disappointment, and still letting the world touch you with joy, even when it felt fleeting. Getting this far has taken everything. Let yourself see this — see you — clearly and without apology.

Thank you for the stubbornness to keep moving, to love even when afraid, to believe in a tomorrow you could not yet see.

Thank you for welcoming all of you: the strong, the tender, the restless, the hurting, the relentless.

Here is what is true: you are not here to stay unchanged. Life will keep asking you to open, to risk, to redraw every line you thought you could not cross. The story of who you are, and where you belong, is still being written.

With every crossing, seen or unseen, you grow a little larger, a little more at home, no matter where you stand.

You have lived in shadow and in light.

You have been claimed by sorrow and by joy.

You have lived within cultures that tried to shape you, and you have shaped them back.

Change is the one certainty. Every border, every loss, every beginning — these are the currents that carried you here. When you tell your story, you make space for it to breathe, to rest, to finally be understood.

This letter, this book, is witness.

It is not a manual but a companion.

It is not only for you. Telling the truth about your life makes it possible for others to walk through their own. This is how we remember: no one is alone in the ache for belonging.

This letter is an offering — born of hard-earned clarity, lit by the hope that anyone wandering, grieving, or reinventing might find warmth here. It is not a slogan. It is a light left on, in case someone else needs to find their way.

For you, and for all of us: this is what persistence looks like.

This is how courage is lived.

This is how we find shelter, again and again — in story, in honesty, in each other.

We are not just getting by. We are shaping the ground we walk on, word by word, day by day, for every version of ourselves, and for anyone who might need a place to land.

May we practise the same kindness with ourselves that we have given away so freely.

May we remember: our stories matter not because they impress, but because they are ours, and they are true.

You do not need approval.

You are not waiting for permission.

You are worthy.

Let yourself be changed.

Let yourself outgrow every border.

Let your heart make its own map.

This is the return.

Remember this — to all that you are, and all you are still becoming.

With love,

The Self Within

Part 1 : THE DEPARTURE

The Call.
The Ache.
The Courage.

Chapter 1

When the Spark Becomes a Portal

The Spark

Leaving your home country is never just about geography. It's about identity. About growth. About surrender.

It starts with something soft, a spark. A glimmer. A gentle voice that says: "There's more for you out there, even if you don't know what it is yet".

Sometimes the spark is loud: a job, a heartbreak, a love story. But often, it begins with something ordinary. For me, it was a zipper pencil pouch with a red double-decker London bus printed on it.

I grew up in Malaysia, in a progressive Muslim household, a place where faith, family, and freedom danced together in complex harmony. I was raised with room to question, to explore, to imagine. But like many Asian daughters, I carried an invisible backpack filled with expectations: be good, honour your family, remember your roots, move with grace.

Even then, something in me reached outward. I don't know where it came from — perhaps it was ancestral, or maybe it was the moment my uncle, Acik Atan, returned from the UK and handed me that pencil pouch. I was six, maybe seven, but I felt like an adult, and I remember something inside me lit up.

That red double decker bus pencil pouch became my North Star. Dreams don't always begin with a bang. Sometimes, they begin with stationery.

Mine began with a spark and the knowing that somewhere out there, a different version of me was waiting to be born. At eighteen, the stars aligned. I made the leap.

My Own Terms

When I landed in London, I headed straight to Regent Street to find that double-decker bus. My friend Hazeline and I spent an entire roll of Kodak film capturing that moment. It wasn't about tourism. It was about arrival, the manifestation of a little girl's dream.

Back then, I thought I'd stay a few years. Decades later, I'm still living away. I've lived in England, Germany, the Netherlands and now France. I've worked across more than forty countries. And I've met so many others like me — people who felt the shift long before the move.

Sometimes, what pushes us isn't discontent. It's the pull of becoming.

We think we're chasing opportunity, but we're really chasing a deeper version of ourselves.

The world at home may be kind, stable, familiar. But something inside nudges: I need more.

That's not rebellion. That's expansion. That's the urge to stretch beyond your origin story.

Not everyone's spark is a pencil pouch. But for many, there's a flicker:

"I want to know what I'm capable of."

"I need space to breathe and become."

"I'm tired of being who everyone expects me to be."

"I want to reinvent myself on my own terms."

The Mind Migrates Too

Long before the suitcase is packed or the ticket is bought, the journey has already begun inside. Something stirs when you close your eyes — an ache not just to leave, but the excitement to become.

Neuroscience calls it novelty bias, the brain's secret hunger for the unfamiliar. Each time we imagine a different horizon or whisper what if, our neurons light up. Tiny sparks of dopamine dance in the mind, internal messengers urging us toward change.

And then comes neuroplasticity, the mind's greatest magic trick: the ability to rewire itself in response to newness.

New cities. New rhythms. New you.

But this transformation is rarely wrapped in fanfare. It slips in disguised as doubt, as the hollow restlessness that follows joy, as the low-grade grief of no longer belonging fully to where you were, nor yet to where you are going.

That unease is not a sign you are lost.

It is evidence you are evolving.

It is your brain carving space for the next version of you.

Every awkward silence in a new language, every unfamiliar street you learn to navigate, every ritual you adopt or release are not just experiences. They are neurons firing, connections forming, pathways building.

You have not lost yourself — you are literally remaking yourself.

Your brain was already migrating.

Your becoming had already begun.

Your body just had not caught the flight yet.

The Leap

The moment came quietly. Not with fireworks or trumpets, but with the stillness that follows a decision already made in the body.

I packed my bags, heart racing with both fear and faith, and boarded a flight that would carry me away from Malaysia, to see the world with my own eyes. But somewhere deep inside, I already knew: life would not return to what it was.

London did not greet me with fanfare. It greeted me with drizzle, grey skies, and a sense of strangeness that seeped into my bones.

Back then, I could not have imagined decades of living away. New deep friendships would form on the move. Lessons stitched across languages and borders.

What I came to learn is that leaving is not just about opportunity. It is about expansion. The pull of becoming. We think we are chasing jobs, studies, love stories. But often we are chasing a deeper version of ourselves.

How Leaving Rewrites You

Leaving resets everything. You don't inherit routines, you build them. From where you shop to how you greet someone, every small choice becomes an act of authorship.

You define your identity without inherited context. You're no longer the daughter of, the friend of, the graduate of. You are simply you. And that can be terrifying. But also freeing.

You learn to do hard things in unfamiliar languages, to build community from scratch, to ask for help without a map. And you begin to see your old life from a distance, not to reject it, but to choose more intentionally. What to keep. What to gently lay down. Even as you grow new branches, your roots remain.

They don't keep you stuck. They keep you grounded.

Reclaiming the Pen

Living abroad strips away autopilot. It asks you to choose again and again who you are becoming.

It's not about running. It's not about rebellion. It's about authorship.

You stop performing the script you were handed and begin writing a story that finally sounds like you.

The Real Journey is Inward

People think the hard part is the distance from familiar places. The infrastructure and the logistics. The paperwork.

But the real journey isn't across borders. The longest distance you'll travel is inside you.

Because when you leave what you know — the culture, the roles, the rhythm — what remains is you. Not the version shaped by expectation. The one waiting underneath.

You begin to ask different questions:

Not "Where am I going?" but "What part of me is ready to emerge?"

And that is where everything changes.

The Little Girl

Sometimes I think about the little girl holding the red pencil pouch. She didn't know what London Heathrow smelled like in the nineties: a mix of sun-warmed citrus, soft coconut and sea salt in the air, mingling with the unmistakable cocktail of foods carried in from across the Commonwealth.

Curries, jerk spices, sweet mango, fried noodles, and unfamiliar herb scents seemed to permeate skins and suitcases, drifting through Terminal 3. It was a scent both chaotic and comforting — a foretaste of how the world would open itself to her.

She didn't know the cost of becoming.

She didn't know that her dream of England would lead her to live in a chateau in Samoreau, to sit in boardrooms in Düsseldorf, to join a baby sign language group in Amsterdam, to wander through canal houses in de Jordaan, to stand on the red dot at a TEDx stage in Rotterdam, or that heartbreak would one day make room for real love.

But she knew more — she knew how to honour her inner voice. She knew how to dream. She knew she wanted more.

I look at my life now, the languages I speak, the daughters I raise, the businesses I have built, the woman I have become, and I know: the girl obsessed with her red pencil pouch would be proud. Not because I did it all correctly. But because I followed the spark. Even when the map disappeared. Even when I felt lost.

I never stopped becoming.

The pouch is gone, somewhere along the many moves. But the girl? She is still here. Not as a reflection of who I am, but as the root that carries me forward, forever entwined with the soil that first held me.

Chapter 2

What We Leave Behind

Goodbye

No matter how ready we are to leave, there is always a goodbye stitched into the lining of departure. Sometimes it is gentle, a home we have outgrown. Often, it is more rupture than release: from family, culture, religion, or even from versions of ourselves we were once taught to love.

We do not talk enough about what we leave behind: the grief, the guilt, the ghosts. We are told to be grateful, to smile, to carry the adventure with grace.

But to leave, even willingly, is to fracture. To split open the self and step into the in-between.

The Unspoken Grief of Migration

You do not just leave your country. You leave your language. Your laughter. Your weather. Your food. You leave the people who just get it.

The shorthand of culture — *lah, ah, eh? a'ah!** — sounds that

* *lah, ah, eh? a'ah!* — The little sounds instead of proper words, to show we are

carry whole worlds of emotion, humour, tension, sarcasm. They rise and fall in rhythm with your breath, like a heartbeat. I underestimated those sounds. I did not know they were the soundtrack of my belonging until I landed somewhere they did not exist.

Three decades on, I now know this: even if your new life is beautiful, there will be moments when you ache for the old one. A familiar smell from your grandmother's kitchen. An old word you have not heard in years that cracks something open in your heart of hearts. The longing for familiarity and simplicity, even when they came wrapped in complexity.

This is grief.

Not because you chose wrongly, but because loss is part of expansion.

The Body Fears the Departure

We do not just leave places. We leave with imprints.

Beneath the excitement of departure, the body begins its own inventory. The nervous system takes notes. The amygdala scans.

Neuroscience calls it separation distress, a primal response baked into our limbic system. Long before passports, we had tribes. And our brain primitively mourns distance.

The smell of fresh curry leaves fried in your grandmother's kitchen. The comfort of being understood without having to explain. These are not luxuries. They are anchors.

When they vanish, your body notices. It sends signals: the ache in your chest, the lump in your throat, the inexplicable tears during a childhood song. This is not weakness. It is your nervous system remembering where safety once lived.

Sometimes it sneaks up on you. Years later, the part of you that longs for continuity still reaches into an old jacket pocket,

---

listening, agreeing or disagreeing, encouraging, or simply keeping rhythm. In many Southeast Asian cultures, these backchanneling noises are a common way to keep conversations warm and flowing without interruption.

checking if the keys to the life you left behind are somehow still there.

Shedding Roles, Wearing New Skins

Leaving is also the quiet death of certain roles. The obedient daughter. The reliable friend. The good child who did not disrupt the flow.

Abroad, you are no longer who you were. You become unanchored from context, and that can feel both liberating and lonely.

You realise some parts of you were survival tactics. Others were stories handed down like heirlooms. Letting them go is a kind of mourning too. But growth does not have to sever love. You can honour your roots without being bound by them. You can outgrow the expectations and still carry the tenderness.

Outgrowing is not betrayal.

It is redefinition.

The Invisible Things We Carry

We do not only pack clothes when we leave. We carry the invisible too. Shame and pride. Family expectation. Ancestral memory. Trauma, both named and silent. And a tender hope that maybe, this new chapter will heal something. And sometimes, if we are lucky, heal something in those who came before us.

I carry with me my only brother, Dzul. Not in my suitcase, but in the hush of my heart I rarely speak about.

Dzul and I were sun-drenched children. He, my reluctant sidekick, often dragged into my role-playing games. I, his fiercest protector. We played, we fought, we reimagined.

I can still hear the echo of his childish laughter, sharp and defiant, chasing me away when he wanted to join his friends on the football field.

And then he went to the Royal Military College, and while he was still there, I left for England.

No farewell ceremony. No dramatic goodbye. Just the quiet erasure of him as I chased my dream.

Even now, it catches in my chest. Not guilt. Not grief. Something deeper. A still ache. It feels like sitting in a room too small for your breath, with ceilings pressing low and the windows shuttered. A place where light should pour in but does not. The ache lives there, familiar yet unspoken.

Maybe I could not let my teenage self feel it then. Maybe to chase the dream, I had to leave the weight behind. But the love never paused. And the tether never snapped.

Every day, half a world away, I carry the brother I left behind. Not in my arms. I carry Dzul not only in memory, but in the marrow of who I am.

The Seloka That Cracks Me Open

I still remember vividly, some years ago, just before **Hari Raya Aidilfitri*, my childhood friend Julie messaged me from Hong Kong. We were both making *rendang*†. I told her I did not have *kerisik*‡. Then she asked, "Are you also listening to Raya songs?"

My favourite is §*Seloka Hari Raya* by Uji Rashid and Hail Amir, a song played across Malaysia during Eid celebrations.

Every year, without fail, when the *takbir*# begins and that song plays —

Selamat Hari Raya, Aidilfitri mulia...

---

* *Hari Raya Aidilfitri* — the joyful Muslim festival at the end of Ramadan, filled with togetherness, forgiveness, new beginnings, and festive foods.

† *Rendang* — a rich, slow-cooked meat dish, lovingly prepared for special occasions, symbolising heritage, patience, and generosity.

‡ *Kerisik* — fragrant toasted coconut, pounded into a paste, adding depth, aroma, and a nutty richness to Malay dishes like *rendang*.

§ *Seloka* — a traditional Malay poetic form, often witty or humorous, used to share wisdom or social commentary.

Takbir — the prayerful chant glorifying God, recited at the close of Ramadan and during Hari Raya, filling mosques and homes with reverence, unity, and celebration.

—it breaks me open. Not out of sadness, but out of a remembering too deep for words.

The cacophony of my mother and her sisters talking over each other, always circling back to their parents' land, interlaced with the smell of *kari ayam**. The familiar discomforts of my mother's annual pre-Raya stress, strangely comforting in their own way. The matching *baju kurung*† . The chaos. The laughter. The joy. The drama. The sticky heat. The everything.

That life feels impossibly far, and still, I ache in Malay during Hari Raya. I ache in the language itself, in its cadences, its laughter, its rhythm — a mother tongue that binds memory to belonging.

You can live differently without disowning where you came from.

You can carry your culture forward.

You can grow new branches without severing your roots.

And sometimes, all it takes is a song. A scent rising from the kitchen. A familiar voice across the sea, wishing, *"Selamat Hari Raya."*‡

Growth is Messy

No one tells you how strange it is to become someone new. To live in-between: no longer who you were, not yet who you are becoming.

Before I left for England, I went to boarding school. A place steeped in pride and promise, but to me it felt like punishment.

* *Kari ayam* — a comforting chicken curry, cooked with spices and coconut milk, a beloved dish in Malay homes and celebrations.

† *Baju kurung* — a traditional Malay outfit of a long tunic and skirt, worn with pride during festivals and formal occasions, symbolising modesty, elegance, and cultural heritage.

‡ *Selamat Hari Raya* — a Malay greeting exchanged during Eid, meaning "Happy Celebration Day," expressing joy, blessing, and togetherness at the close of Ramadan.

Nestled in the middle of nowhere, in the small town of Raub, it was meant to shape us into something larger. To me, it felt like being shrunk, as if I had been forced into clothes two sizes too small. Tight, uncomfortable, suffocating – a poor fit for who I really was.

The smell of chalk dust in the classrooms. The stiff uniforms. The chalky canvas shoes. The silencing of my inner voice. I hated it. Not like a child hates spinach. More like a soul displaced from its source.

And yet, in that unfamiliar landscape, I began to learn what I would need to feel at home. I needed connection. The rare warmth of being seen. That is when Yana came into my life.

Yana did not rescue me. She borrowed my *baju kurung*. And in the margins of that place, we stitched a friendship that saved us both. We did silly things, like drinking Coca-Cola mixed with paracetamol, thinking it rebellious and funny. It never gave us a high, but it gave us a secret. And we earned ourselves a story for life when Yana fell ill from it, our mischief discovered, and we were sent to detention. A ritual of defiance that felt like freedom in a place that wanted to press us into silence. We laughed, not because it made sense, but because it was ours.

We saw each other not for who we were supposed to become, but for who we already were. In Yana's companionship, I tasted what it meant to belong. Not to a place, but to a person who recognised me without asking me to change.

And then there was *Cikgu** Fauziah, my English teacher. She had studied in England and returned to teach at our little school in the back of beyond. In the plainness of that small town, she was a kind of rockstar in my teenage eyes. I was in awe of her confident strut along the corridors in high heels, her voice echoing with authority. She was my idol. Her presence carried light. She made

---

* *Cikgu* – the Malay word for teacher. In Malaysia, teachers are respectfully called *Cikgu* (rather than just their names) because teaching is seen as an honourable role, and the title shows gratitude as well as respect.

me feel seen in a way the rules could not erase. She noticed my untameable spirit, even when I tried to dim it.

Cikgu Fauziah did more than inspire me; she carved a path for me to walk. She groomed me to become the captain of the school's English debating team. That stage, those arguments, that microphone in my hand became an outlet for a voice that Raub had tried to silence. For the first time, I saw a thread connecting who I was then to who I might become.

Those two — Yana with her comforting nature and *Cikgu* Fauziah with her steady recognition of the spark I carried — reminded me that belonging was never about place. It was about people who could see you and still hold you.

That is when it began. The first quiet bricks of a home within. Not built in safety, but in connection. Not in comfort, but in someone seeing me as I was, even as I was still becoming.

My five years in Raub never made me feel at home. But I know now that sometimes the hard places are not detours. They are doorways. Doorways into unexpected friendships, mentors, and glimpses of the future self already stirring inside you.

Integration is the Real Work

Eventually, you begin to weave.

The old with the new.

What you will carry. What you will set down.

You realise you are not trying to go back — you cannot.

You are not even trying to belong the way you used to.

You are building a home that travels with you.

One that holds the full story. Not the filtered one.

The real one.

And the thread that keeps it together is always connection.

A Burger Called Freedom

If the feeling of leaving my motherland had a nostalgic flavour, it would not be my Malaysian favourite, *char kway teow*.* Strangely enough, it would be something more international, like a burger.

Glossy bun. Cheese melting. Promise wrapped in waxy paper. But take a bite, and it surprises you: heat you did not expect, pickles that punch, grease that lingers.

That is what leaving Malaysia tastes like.

At Subang airport, I looked like the top bun: glossy, bold, full of hope. But I was also carrying the fine print. My father, half-joking: "If your grades slip and a man asks for your hand, I'll marry you off."

The taste of freedom came with conditions. Still, I bit into it. And with every bite of my proverbial burger, I was transforming.

Holding the contradiction with both hands. Performing two lives at once. Flirting with freedom. Remembering the rules.

Today, whenever I see a girl eating a burger, I remember the bites that teenager took, carrying ancestral weight and joy. The taste of something she was not sure she'd ever reach. And even there, in the contradiction, I craved connection: a place where freedom and belonging could sit at the same table.

The Brain Craves a Map

The mind wants to belong, but it seeks patterns, not poetry. It wants to know when to speak, when to pause, how to read the room.

Back home, you knew the script like muscle memory. But abroad, your brain scrambles. It scans for the rules. This is neuro-

---

* *Char Kway Teow* — a famous Malaysian stir-fried noodle dish made with flat rice noodles, soy sauce, prawns, egg, bean sprouts, and sometimes cockles and Chinese sausage, cooked over high heat for a smoky, charred flavour.

plasticity in action, not in theory — your brain trying to build a map where none exists.

So you adapt. You shift your tone. You soften the verbs. You make your warmth smaller. Or louder. This is not inauthentic. This is survival. This is stretch. This is becoming multilingual in the language of emotion.

And slowly, you realise: you are no longer looking for the old map. You are the compass now.

Belonging is not the Same as Fitting In

You overthink everything. Too much? Too little? Too formal? Too relaxed?

You realise that generosity looks different here. So does humour. So does love.

You begin to unlearn your instincts, not because they are wrong, but because they no longer translate. What once flowed naturally now requires rehearsal. And just when you think you have cracked the code, life might move you again.

New rules.

New codes.

New confusion.

In that stretch comes the loss of ease. The grief of not being known. The ache of becoming new.

This is the paradox of migration: you must first be disoriented before you can reorient. You lose fluency in yourself before you find a deeper version of who you are. It is only in the wilderness of not-belonging that you begin to sense what belonging really means.

Which is why the smallest acts of connection matter so deeply. A smile across a crowded room. A shared meal offered without hesitation. Someone saying your name with care.

These are not small things. They are lifelines. They tether you when everything else feels untranslatable.

And slowly, you realise that fitting in is about performance, but belonging is about presence. Fitting in asks you to wear clothes that pinch at the seams. Belonging allows you to exhale into something made for your skin. One is camouflage. The other is home.

Becoming the New You

When you leave, you do not just lose place.

You lose the person you were in that place.

The one who knew how to navigate.

The one fluent in her own skin.

You become a beginner again.

At first you wonder if you have made a mistake. The hollow ache of being out of step in every conversation.

But what feels like breaking is actually the slow work of becoming.

You must first be disoriented before you can reorient.

You must first lose your bearings before you can learn to trust a deeper compass.

And in that wilderness, something shifts. You stretch. You soften. You learn to hold nuance, to read silence, to sit in ambiguity.

You begin to find connection not in the old scripts, but in the smallest human gestures.

A smile.

A shared joke.

The warmth of someone who sees you without translation.

These moments remind you that belonging was never about fitting in. It was always about being seen.

Slowly, you build a rhythm.

A new self. Not diluted. Expanded.

Not fully from here. Not fully from there.

But rooted in resilience, and in the connections that hold you.

Because every time it hits you — that feeling of being lost — you are not failing.

You are still becoming.

Not broken. Just new.

To leave is never only to go. It is to lose yourself just enough to find yourself again. It is to become, to grow new roots where you once thought you could not.

Chapter 3

In Between Worlds

Not Quite This, Not Quite That

No one tells you that when you leave your country, you might also leave behind your place in the world. It's not that you stop existing. It's that you start floating. Between cultures. Between languages. Between selves.

You return home and something feels off. You don't laugh at the same jokes. You stumble through silences woven with social codes. People say, *"Wah, so different now ah?!"* — and the words do not always carry admiration.

You go back abroad and something is missing. The food is never quite right. You crave *sambal**, not sandwiches. You long for someone who can read the meaning of your backchanneling sigh without translation.

* *Sambal* — a fragrant chilli paste made from a blend of chillies, garlic, shallots, lime, shrimp paste, and sometimes calamansi citrus, tomatoes, or tamarind, pounded into a fiery relish. In the Malay archipelago, it is more than food — it is memory, it is emotion. Every family has its own *sambal*, slightly different in texture, heat, or sweetness, passed down like an heirloom. It accompanies the simplest rice as faithfully as it crowns a feast, carrying the comfort of home, the warmth of gatherings, and the taste of belonging itself.

You are not fully of here. You are no longer fully of there. This is the ache of the in-between.

What Does It Mean to Belong?

Belonging is a slippery thing. It refuses to stay in one definition, one geography, one face.

Sometimes it means being known — surrounded by people who can read your story without preamble, who understand the rhythm of your silences as much as your words.

Other times it means being seen — recognised not for who you were but for who you are becoming, even before you have fully arrived.

For those of us who have crossed oceans and cultures, belonging shifts shape. It is less a treasure to stumble upon and more a temple we learn to build with our own hands.

It becomes less about location and more about liberation. Not the postcode or the passport, but the spaciousness to bring your whole self to the table without disguise, and the creative force to imagine who you might still become.

Perhaps belonging is not a final destination at all, but a practice.

A daily architecture of presence and permission.

A quiet vow we make to ourselves: I will not abandon who I am, even if I do not yet know the full story of who I will be.

For me, this is the most magical part: that identity does not demand certainty, but welcomes mystery. That I can stand at the edge of myself, unfinished, and still feel at home.

To belong is not to know everything, but to trust that even in the unknowing, I am still becoming.

Belonging is a Muscle

It is not binary. You don't either belong or not. It is a muscle. It grows where you feed it.

You find little altars of belonging in unexpected corners. Like the Chinese restaurant on Carl-Bertelsmann Straße in Gütersloh, where my colleague Honour and I became lunchtime regulars.

Honour was American — svelte, sharp-witted, a long-distance runner who lived her life the way she ran her miles: steady, resilient, never giving up at the first hill.

The waitress soon stopped asking. She would tilt her head and smile: *"Zwei mal, Nummer Eins mit Tofu, ohne Ei?"* Two portions of number one with tofu, no egg. And we would answer in unison, *"Ja, bitte."* Yes, please. Every single time.

It became our ritual. A rhythm of belonging in a place that often felt foreign to both of us — her from across the Atlantic, me from across the South China Sea. We laughed at the predictability of it, joked about our culinary loyalty, and in the small act of repetition, we stitched a kind of home.

Honour would often remind me that belonging, like running, was built step by step. Some days you glide, others you ache, but you keep going until the path feels like your own. That simple wisdom carried me further than she realised.

And then there was Marco. Half German, half Italian, he carried both with grace — the pragmatism of one, the warmth and humour of the other. He appeared like a brother you didn't know you needed, always ready with a calm word or a mischievous grin.

When my car was impounded, panic caught at my breath. Marco, unbothered, leaned in and told me to smile sweetly, to play the *"Ich bin Ausländerin — I'm just a foreign lady"* card. *"Trust me,"* he said, *"it almost always works."*

... and it did. My car was released, fine-free.

Later that evening, in a tiny *Stube**, the very same policeman, now off duty and tipsy, recognised me and tried to dance with me

* *Stube* — in Germany, a cosy, traditional room or small pub, usually wood-lined, where people gather to eat, drink, and socialise. A place where laughter and familiarity soften the edges of the day.

on the cramped wooden floor. I didn't recognise him at first. I turned away.

Marco roared with laughter. *"You were all sweetness and survival at the station,"* he said, *"and then you left him dancing alone. You, naughty Asian chick!"* We laughed until our stomachs ached.

Belonging, I realised, speaks many dialects. And apparently, dancing with off-duty policemen is not one of mine. But these moments — the tofu rituals with Honour, the absurd impound drama with Marco, the teasing and the tenderness — slowly softened the sharp edges of my outsider status.

I began to see that behind the serious exteriors, Germans were often hilarious, deeply kind, and loyal to the bone. And slowly, I started to take a new shape — and not shrink.

Because, as Honour often reminded me, belonging is like running. It is not about speed, but stamina. It is the quiet courage to keep showing up, step after step, until one day the road itself begins to feel like home.

Gathering Contrast

London's multicultural tide once let me blend in. In Gütersloh, Germany, I could not. I was the brown woman in the supermarket queue. The only Asian in many meetings. The one with an accent. It made me hyper-aware of my presence. But it also forced me to make peace with being seen.

After ten years in England, my tongue had been schooled in understatement. Every sentence was softened by politeness, padded with suggestion. I had learned to speak in codes, never quite naming a thing, but circling it with care. *"Perhaps we could consider..." "Would it be possible..."* Indirection was the language of belonging.

Germany was a different song. My gentle spirals of speech met with *"Ja oder nein?"* Yes or no. Direct. Immediate.

At first, it felt like a clash. My British nuance crumbled

against German bluntness. But slowly, I began to see it not as conflict but as contrast, like two instruments in the same orchestra — different in tone, yet capable of harmony.

The English say, *"Silence is golden."*

The Germans say, *"Klare Worte sind ein Freundschaftsdienst"** — clear words serve friendships.

One treasures quiet diplomacy, the other honours plain truth. And in their difference, both hold beauty.

Migration taught me to bend between them. To know when to cushion my words with courtesy, and when to place them sharp and simple, like crystal on a table. There was freedom in both: the warmth of subtlety, the strength of clarity.

And as I adapted, I did not become someone else. I became more. A self fluent in contrasts. A woman who could dance between understatement and directness, between the English art of suggestion and the German gift of precision.

Belonging is not about choosing one language of being. More often than not, even if your migration is not geographical but emotional or intellectual, the sense of belonging is about gathering contrasts — and letting them remake you into something larger, richer, and more whole.

When the Room Did Not Look Like Me

I remember the spotlights. Bright. Unforgiving. They pressed heavy on my shoulders, making the stage feel both vast and intimate at once.

It was 2012, the very first Rockstart Accelerator in Amsterdam. The venue was tucked in NDSM†, then a raw industrial quarter by the water. Not the polished Amsterdam of postcards,

---

* *"Klare Worte sind ein Freundschaftsdienst"* — a German proverb meaning "clear words serve friendships." It reflects a cultural value that honesty, even if blunt, is seen as a gesture of care.

† *NDSM* — a former shipyard in Amsterdam Noord, later transformed into a cultural hub with artist studios, cafés, and event spaces. Known for its raw, indus-

but a place alive with edges: graffiti on concrete walls, echoes of shipbuilding, warehouses reborn as playgrounds for broke, bright-eyed founders, artists, and dreamers running on caffeine and possibility. It wasn't glossy. It was gritty. And it was electric.

And there I stood on that stage, the only female CEO in the entire cohort.

Not just the only woman.

The only brown woman.

Not yet 40.

Not from Stanford, Harvard, or Oxford.

Not carrying the easy weight of trust-fund capital or legacy networks.

I stood beside my two young Latvian co-founders, Artis and Arturs, who carried their own kind of fire. Together we had built something bold, imperfect, alive. And I was not just the face of it. I had invested in it. Expanded it to Malaysia. Carried its risk in my bones and its vision in my voice.

This was not performance. This was stake.

This was skin.

This was story carried in my bones.

In that moment, I felt two worlds collide: the woman under the hot Amsterdam lights, and the little girl in Malaysia who once held a red zipper pencil pouch with a London bus printed on it, dreaming of elsewhere.

I was not there to prove anything. Not to be a banner for women, or migrants, or mothers. I was there for something simpler, something harder: self-belief.

To stand in a room that had never looked like me, and still know I belonged. To remind myself that background is not baggage. That standing out is not an apology. That every fragment of my lived experience — every migration, heartbreak, and reinvention — had a right to stand tall in that room.

---

trial character and graffiti-covered warehouses, it became a symbol of reinvention and creative grit.

The applause was loud, but it was not what mattered. What mattered was the rhythm of my own heartbeat: steady, insistent, more precious than recognition. A home within.

One not created by clapping hands, but by all that had shaped me: fear and courage, selflessness and selfishness, heartbreak and rebuilding, ambition and tenderness, exile and motherhood. In the sound of my own heartbeat, I heard a home far larger than the little girl from Malaysia had ever dared to imagine, even in her boldest daydreams.

The spotlight was intense, but I realised it was never meant to be my only light. What carried me was the softer flame I had kindled inside, a light not dependent on permission, but on presence.

And perhaps that is the gift of living between worlds: you are never entirely of one place, nor entirely of another. You carry your own lamp, burning steady in the middle space.

In between is not emptiness.

In between is expansion.

In between is where the light of who you were meets the light of who you are becoming.

And that, I have learned, that in between is where life dances with me.

The Larger Space

People love to ask, *"So, where are you from?"* For those of us between worlds, it is never a one-word answer.

Some ask it with innocent curiosity. Others ask it with a gaze that quietly says, *"You don't belong here."* But perhaps the hardest moments are when you turn the question inward and hear yourself whisper the same thing.

Neuroscience tells us why. The brain is wired for categories, always scanning for where we fit. Our ancestors survived by sensing who was in the tribe and who was not, by reading accents, faces, gestures. To be outcast once meant danger. And so, even today, our nervous system still flinches when belonging feels uncertain.

The amygdala*, that small almond-shaped centre of vigilance, lights up when we feel different. The body tightens. Breath shortens. We search for safety in labels and identities, because clarity calms the mind.

But the gift of migration — of being between worlds — is that the brain can also stretch. Neuroplasticity† is the river's way of carving new pathways. It allows us to rewire old reflexes, to learn that safety does not always come from sameness.

Belonging can be redefined, not as conformity, but as coherence: the quiet alignment of who we are with what we believe, and how we choose to live.

It is a slow practice. A daily retraining of the nervous system. To stand in unfamiliar circles and remind yourself: my story is still valid here. My presence is still worthy here.

In time, the question shifts from accusation to invitation. *"Where are you from?"* becomes less about proving coordinates, and more about honouring the mosaic of places and people that live inside you.

And the answer, even if it is long, even if it is layered, becomes not just an explanation, but a new kind of space. A space large enough to hold all the different layers of you.

The Beauty of Non-Belonging

There is a strange gift in not fitting perfectly anywhere.

At first it feels like fracture, like standing in a doorway that

---

* *Amygdala* — an almond-shaped structure deep in the brain, part of the limbic system. It plays a key role in emotional processing, especially fear and vigilance. When belonging feels uncertain, the amygdala activates as if detecting danger, even in modern contexts.

† *Neuroplasticity* — the brain's ability to form and reorganise connections in response to experience. Like a river carving new channels, it allows us to adapt, heal, and grow new ways of being even after rupture.

never fully opens. But over time, the doorway becomes a threshold, and you begin to see what others cannot.

You learn to listen for the unspoken. You become fluent in nuance, sensitive to the tremor in a voice, the pause between words, the way silence can carry more truth than speech.

You build empathy in your bones. You learn to hold contradictions without needing to solve them. You begin to see the world not in absolutes, but in gradients. In the beauty of the blur.

Like ink dissolving in water, identities blend and re-form, and you learn to rest in the mystery of becoming.

When life breaks you into fragments, it is because you are ready to be put back together differently. Every piece of you that feels disconnected is a piece that will find a new place, a new purpose, a new meaning. And sometimes, in our messiness, we find our greatest wholeness.

We find the courage to rebuild, to reimagine, to redefine what it means to be ourselves.

You are never broken; you are breaking through.

And if you are both lucky and courageous, you begin to write your own story in the process of putting the puzzle into a new picture. Not the one others expect of you, but the one that grows slowly, like moss across stone — tender and resilient.

A picture and a story not made of coordinates or categories, but of self-created presence.

And perhaps that is the quiet gift of not belonging: the freedom to realise you were never meant to fit into one shape, but to keep unfolding into your own unique shape.

To belong everywhere, you must first learn to sit peacefully with not belonging at all.

The Home Never Leaves

Eventually, the ache softens. What once felt like fracture begins to feel like space. You start to notice the ground beneath your feet, even if you are still figuring out the map.

You understand that home is not always where you began. Sometimes it is the place where you became who you are.

And sometimes, most sacred of all, it is who you are when no one is watching.

Neuroscience tells us our sense of self is braided together through memory and repetition. Each time we pause, breathe, and choose presence, the brain lays down new pathways, reminding us: here too, you belong. Here too, you are safe. Belonging is not only recognition from others; it is the nervous system remembering that your own company can be a place of rest.

Zen wisdom offers the same truth more simply: *"Wherever you go, there you are."** Sit in stillness long enough, and you will notice that you carry the entire house of your becoming — with all its quiet rooms and open windows — within you.

You discover that home can be as effortless as a single breath, as ordinary as the ritual of tea, as vast as the silence that greets you when you finally stop searching for your place in the world.

Coming home to yourself is not an arrival but a practice. Some days it feels like ease; other days, like a tender negotiation with your own restless heart. Yet with each return, you learn that you do not need to wait for permission, or for a place to welcome you.

You may forget it at times, but home has never left you.

Shifting Multitudes

The mind is not made for stillness. It leans toward change. Each time we step into the unfamiliar, it reshapes itself, learning, stretching, growing into new possibility.

A different routine, a clash of cultures, the awkward search for words in a new language — all of it stirs the mind awake. What

---

* *"Wherever you go, there you are"* — a phrase often linked to Zen and Buddhist traditions, reminding us that home is found not in place, but in presence. Popularised in modern mindfulness, it captures the truth that self-belonging travels with us.

feels like disorientation on the surface is, at a deeper level, the self widening its horizons.

Uncertainty has a way of tightening the chest and crowding the mind. Yet it also carries hidden generosity. It teaches us to bend instead of break. To live outside the predictable is to strengthen our capacity for flexibility, both of thought and of heart.

African wisdom* holds it this way: *"Wisdom is like a baobab tree; no one individual can embrace it."* To stretch beyond what is familiar is to gather more branches, more roots, more shades of understanding.

The stretch itself becomes wisdom. To carry sorrow without drowning in it. To cradle joy without clutching at it. To let doubt and wonder sit side by side at the same table.

And somewhere in that widening, identity loosens its grip. It stops insisting on one label, one shape, one story. It becomes more fluid. More spacious.

You learn you do not have to be either this or that.

You are allowed to be many things at once.

You grow to contain multitudes.

The Unknown Rewires Us

To step into the unknown is to stretch the edges of who we think we are. And not every change arrives neatly written on a vision board.

Some changes crash in like waves, fast and loud, impossible to resist. Others slip in quietly, disguised as boredom, a restless body, or an idea you can no longer unsee. However it arrives, real change always asks us to surrender control. And that surrender can feel like chaos.

---

* *Akan proverb* — "Wisdom is like a baobab tree; no one individual can embrace it." In Ghanaian tradition, the baobab symbolises community knowledge: wisdom is collective, never owned by one alone.

That is how my move to Amsterdam began. A gentle unravelling of the life I had known, and a slow weaving of one I had not expected.

Change brought life, in every sense of the word. And with it came the role I had never trained for: a new mother in a foreign land. And becoming a parent while navigating a new country brings the in-between to an entirely new level.

You are holding more than one culture in your hands, and now, a child in your arms. You are figuring out your own identity while shaping another's.

And deep inside, the ambition does not quiet down. You still want to build, to lead, to become. The pull of creation continues, even as your body and your days are claimed by care. It is disorienting — and yet it is defining.

History reminds us that change often arrives before we are ready.

On the night of 9 November 1989, crowds gathered in Berlin as the Wall that had divided a city, a country, and the world for almost three decades began to crumble. Families crossed from East to West. Soldiers, once guardians of separation, stood bewildered as the impossible unfolded before their eyes. Within hours, what had seemed permanent was gone.

Angela Merkel, who would later become Germany's first female Chancellor, once said: *"The fall of the Berlin Wall is testimony to the fact that dreams can be stronger than walls."* *

For Berliners, that night was chaos and possibility braided together. They had to rebuild not only their lives but their sense of self. To step into a future with no script, to become citizens of a story that had only just begun.

In my own way, Amsterdam was my Berlin Wall moment. A

* *Berlin Wall, 1989* — On 9 November, crowds dismantled the barrier that had divided East and West Berlin for nearly 30 years. Its fall became a global symbol of freedom and reinvention. Angela Merkel is Germany's first female Chancellor and a former East Berliner.

reconstruction of what I thought life would be, and the slow, fragile building of something unexpected.

I had to start again — something that looked easy, but never was as I had imagined. I had to find people to lean on in unexpected places, even in a baby sign language class where strangers became a kind of tribe.

At the same time, I stepped into startup spaces, scale-up teams, and digital playgrounds. These were unfamiliar territories where I had to grow a new kind of confidence — one that made room for both my ambition and my motherhood.

Being a mother in a foreign land made me more direct. More focused. More grounded in what I knew, and more comfortable in what I did not.

And to my surprise, I did not just adjust. I evolved.

That, I realised, is how the home within grows. Because home is not always something you return to. Sometimes, it is something you become.

If your life has taken a turn you never planned for — if you are mothering, mentoring, managing, migrating. If you are standing in a role, a country, or a season that feels unfamiliar — this chapter of your life may not look like your vision board. But it may be the blueprint for a self you never dared to dream into being.

Let it shape you. Let it soften you.

And let it remind you: you can build home anywhere. Start wherever you are in your journey.

Novelties and Sparks

The mind loves patterns. Familiar faces. Predictable endings.

So when life shifts into a new country, a new role, or a new version of self, the nervous system lights up in protest. Not because it is wrong, but because it is unknown.

The amygdala, that small inner alarm, whispers: *This is unsafe.*

What it really means is: *This is unfamiliar.*

The gift is in staying. In breathing through the static. In allowing the wiser part of the mind — the prefrontal cortex* — to step forward and remind us: *We are safe. This is new, not dangerous.*

That is where rewiring begins.

Novelty is not just exciting. It is transformative.

Each time you try something new — whether speaking a word in another tongue, walking down an unfamiliar street, or sitting with an emotion you once avoided — the brain forges fresh connections.

Dopamine sparks. Curiosity stirs. New maps unfold inside you.

And little by little, you change.

You are not only adjusting.

You are becoming.

Neuroscience calls this plasticity. I call it the quiet architecture of becoming.

Heraclitus† said it long ago: *"No man ever steps in the same river twice, for it is not the same river and he is not the same man."*

We were never meant to stay the same.

And novelty, however small, is the spark that keeps the inner fire alive.

Painful Crossings

Let's be honest: growth rarely feels good in real time.It is awkward. Tender. Sometimes terrifying.

But discomfort is not the enemy. It is the doorway.

---

* *Amygdala and prefrontal cortex* — The amygdala scans for threat and fuels fear, while the prefrontal cortex governs reasoning, choice, and calm. Together, they illustrate how novelty can feel unsafe but also open pathways for growth.

† *Heraclitus* — a Greek philosopher (c. 500 BCE) who taught that change is the essence of life. His river metaphor endures as a reminder that transformation is not failure, but the flow of existence itself.

It is what stretches our emotional muscles and deepens our range.

That shaky first step.

That lump in your throat.

That pang of self-doubt.

All of it is the body's way of saying: *You are expanding.*

I know this in my bones. In 2017, our younger daughter Isabel was diagnosed with Trip12, a rare genetic disorder. At the time, she was one of only twenty-one children in the world with that diagnosis.

The doctors knew very little about it, and there were no other parents we could turn to for guidance or hope. We felt helpless. We felt in the dark.

My whole life tilted in the middle of that rainy Dutch spring day. It was cold, grey, grim and wet. It felt like my entire life was soaked with extreme sadness.

I did not know who I was becoming, and I did not know where I was heading. The map dissolved in my hands, and I was left standing in a wilderness I had never imagined for myself or for my child.

The Stoic philosopher Seneca wrote, *"Difficulties strengthen the mind, as labour does the body."* At the time, I could not see strength. All I felt was rupture. Yet what unsettles us is often what prepares us.

In many African traditions, initiation rites are built around discomfort, not as punishment but as passage. Pain and uncertainty mark the threshold between what was and what will be. Hardship becomes the portal to wisdom.

Looking back now, I see that diagnosis as one of my initiations. It was a passage I did not choose, yet one that reshaped me entirely. I had to grow new patience, new humility, new resilience.

And today, here I am, writing this book, telling this story, proof that even in the darkest discomfort, new life can take root.

If you can stay with it, even a little longer, you emerge more grounded, more honest, more yourself.

Between the comfort of what you knew and the clarity of who you are becoming lies this space of unease.

It is not emptiness. It is expansion. Discomfort is not proof that you are lost. It is the sign that you are already crossing into new ground.

I am reminded again and again, in between is a good place to be.

The Wonder of In-Between

There is a quiet power in uncertainty. In releasing the need to have everything mapped out.

Because when we loosen our grip, we create space for what we could not have planned. Space for redirection, for grace, for the unimagined to arrive.

This is not about rushing through or bypassing the hard parts. It is about staying awake in the messy middle, trusting that the mess itself is part of the alchemy of growth.

The mystics have always known this. Rainer Maria Rilke once wrote: *"Be patient toward all that is unsolved in your heart and try to love the questions themselves."* To live in wonder is to honour the questions, to sit with what is unfinished, to let possibility ripen in its own time.*

Migration, motherhood, reinvention — all of it is uncertain. All of it reshapes us. And yet uncertainty is not emptiness. It is fertile ground. It is where the old self softens, and the new one begins to take root.

When Isabel was diagnosed, I could not imagine light on the other side of that news. I did not know who I was becoming, nor where the road would lead. And yet, even there, in the darkest

* Rainer Maria Rilke (1875–1926), the Bohemian-Austrian poet and mystic, is best known for his *Letters to a Young Poet*, where he urged readers to embrace uncertainty and "love the questions." His work continues to inspire those navigating transformation, reminding us that the unfinished and unresolved can be a source of beauty and becoming.

unknown, wonder still found me. Slowly. Through love, through resilience, through the unexpected gift of writing these words today.

When we resist the unknown, we close ourselves off to surprise. But when we live with open hands, even the most ordinary day can shimmer: a child's laugh, a stranger's kindness, the simple miracle of being here, still becoming.

So let yourself live in wonder.

Let yourself marvel at the way you are being reshaped, even when it feels untidy.

Because the truth is this:

you do not have to arrive anywhere to belong.

The in-between is not the failure of certainty.

The in-between is the place of wonder.

Chapter 4

Holding On & Letting Go

Rooting Without a Map

When you move — really move — not just your body but your entire way of being, something begins to unravel. You don't mean for it to happen.

I packed my bags with the best of intentions: notebooks, a stash of asam laksa Maggi Mee*, a photo of my family, and a few saga seeds† I had treasured since childhood, playing with my best friend Wa beneath the school gate on Jalan Gurney.

I carried my ambitions. My polished self-introduction. My incomplete ideas of who I was. And a grand plan, in my head.

But life in a new place has a way of softening the edges you once called identity. Unless your degree comes stamped with an expensive crest from Harvard or Oxford, it barely registers.

I see this in the way David, my French husband, tells people

---

* *Asam laksa Maggi Mee* — for Malaysians, more than instant noodles. A portable taste of home, a bowl of comfort that travels anywhere.

† *Saga seeds* — bright red "love seeds" that children in Malaysia and Singapore collect, exchange, and treasure as tokens of friendship.

he went to *la grande école*[*]. In France, the phrase is a badge of belonging. In the Netherlands, it sounds more like he's bragging about finishing high school[†].

And the whole *"Do you know who she is?"* thing? That vanishes the moment your plane touches down in the West. Back home in Malaysia, names and lineages open doors. Abroad, no one cares. Nepotism does not translate across borders.

Especially if you come from a developing country, you start from zero. The car you drove, the family you came from, the title on your business card — none of it carries weight here. Merit matters. Reputation is earned, not inherited.

Your jokes don't land. Your references evaporate in translation. The scaffolding that once made you legible falls away. And this is where growth begins — in the quiet art of letting go.

Trust in Chemistry

Letting go does not always begin with intention. Sometimes it starts with erosion.

In a new country, the scaffolding of self begins to dissolve. The credentials you carried like armour are unread. The reputation you built is erased by a postcode change. The cultural shorthand that once made you familiar now lands like a foreign tongue.

At first, you try to prove yourself. You arrive with stories of what you've built, where you've worked, what you've led. And you are met with silence.

I was convinced I would impress my French in-laws with my debutante sophistication. I had studied French in Fontainebleau for nine months — ten years before I even met my husband, but surely linguistic talent ages like wine. I could name four kinds of

---

* *Les Grandes Écoles* — France's elite universities, highly selective and seen as gateways to leadership in business, politics, and science.

† The Netherlands — in contrast, Dutch education is egalitarian, and society values humility and practicality. Status comes less from where you studied, more from what you do.

cheese, which felt like an achievement for a Malaysian woman raised on cheddar. And I could say *enchantée* with what I fancied was Parisienne ease.

What I received instead were long silences, polite nods, and the raised eyebrow of an invisible social exam. It turns out, my rehearsed sophistication was less *chic* and more enthusiastic tourist with a cheese vocabulary. They were not being unkind. They were being French* — reserved, private, masters of subtext. For years, I felt as though I was failing.

What I learned is that adaptation is not only about language. It is about releasing expectations of what connection should look like. I learned to let time do the work. To stop proving. To trust that what was meant for me would never miss me.

The brain rewires not just through the passing of days, but through the quality of them: moments of gentle connection, clarity, and the absence of threat. Each time you choose not to chase, not to beg, not to force, you give your nervous system space to exhale. Cortisol eases. Dopamine steadies. The body stops bracing for impact.

This too is chemistry.

Spiritual Unpacking

There is a second kind of unpacking when you arrive in a new place. Not the suitcase, but the self.

You open the bag of invisible things — expectations, inherited scripts, quiet *shoulds* stitched into your upbringing. You hold them up to the light. Some still bless you. Some no longer fit. Some never belonged to you at all.

In Malay we say: *buang yang keruh, ambil yang jernih* —

* French culture often reserved and layered with subtext. Politeness, privacy, and understatement are valued, which can feel like distance to outsiders but carry their own quiet codes of connection.

discard the murky, keep what is clear. Migration insists you practise this not as philosophy but as survival.

Because abroad, the scaffolding that once defined you does not translate. Status, family name, social codes — all evaporate. What remains is yourself, stripped of applause. It can feel like loss, but it is also a rare chance.

This is the slow labour of migration: not just adding new layers, but loosening old skins that no longer let you breathe. Not betraying your roots, but pruning them so the tree of you can grow taller, freer.

It is not glamorous work. It will not trend on Instagram. It is lonely at times, like sitting on the floor with a pile of old letters, deciding which still carry truth and which must be released. Yet it is this quiet pruning that makes space for new growth.

And in that space, resilience begins. Not toughness, but clarity. The clarity to know what is worth carrying, and what is safe to lay down.

Red, White and KLM Blue

To arrive in a new place is to agree, silently and sometimes unwillingly, to meet yourself again in unfamiliar colours.

You begin to do things not for recognition, but because they feel right. You grow curious about the new shades of life.

I remember arriving in Amsterdam, thinking I would find my footing quickly. After all, I had adapted before. In Germany I found my way with surprising ease. At twenty-nine, in full stride, directing projects across Europe, my calendar was full, my name spoken in rooms that mattered. I belonged to a structure that desired me, and that desire mirrored me back to myself.

But Amsterdam was different. I did not arrive as a professional. I arrived as a partner. As a mother. There was no onboarding, no inbox, no one waiting for my opinion. Only sleepless nights with a newborn. Hairdressers who turned my hair orange.

Mama groups where I could not quite translate my warmth. Dutch small talk that cut sharper than I expected.

Gone was the woman who negotiated licensing deals across countries. In her place stood someone I did not yet recognise, scrambling inside a new identity.

It did not feel beautiful at the time.

It felt like discomfort.

Because when you have been seen through titles and roles, you forget who you are without them. And when those roles fall away, it is disorienting. No one tells you how long it might take to feel like yourself again. You are not behind.

You are on sacred, untamed time.

And in that in-between, where you are no longer who you were but not yet who you are becoming, you find something gentler than confidence. You find truth. You practise self-tenderness. You begin, piece by piece, to anchor in who you are — not in the world's reflection, but in your own inner knowing.

What I learned in that slow season is this: you cannot hold yourself to the same timeline when your circumstances are radically different.

And when identity shifts alongside place, the ground does not only move beneath you. It moves within you.

There is no map for this kind of becoming. Only the rawness of truth and the grace to keep going. No title to hold onto. Just the unfamiliar weight of your new layers.

So give yourself time.

Give your new context time.

A life arranged in quiet layers: red, white, and KLM blue*. Over time, you may learn to love these colours. Not as a flag, but

* *KLM Blue* — the vivid cobalt colour of the Dutch national airline, Koninklijke Luchtvaart Maatschappij (KLM). Since 1919, its distinctive blue planes have symbolised both Dutch identity and the promise of journeys across borders. For many, it is the first colour seen when arriving in or leaving the Netherlands — a shade that quietly weaves itself into the migrant's palette of belonging.

as the tender shades of fresh skin, joining all the other colours stretched across the inner walls of your home within.

The Altar of Presence

When the familiar scaffolds fall away, what holds you?

For some, it is religion. For others, the quieter tools of the inner life. For me, a bit of both.

I began to carry a notebook and pencil everywhere, scribbling reminders to myself — tender words I did not yet know would one day become companions for others walking the same rare path.

I discovered sweaty Bikram yoga, where my body poured out the racing thoughts that would not leave me. I whispered silent du'as[*], not in the exact way I was taught at the *surau*[†] Al-Khairiah, but in the quiet knowing that connection to the Divine is never severed, even in Amsterdam.

I walked barefoot across the unfamiliar grass in Sarphatipark. Softer, wetter, nothing like the dry scratch of home. My ten-month-old chewed happily on sand in the *zandbak*[‡], her grin wide with satisfaction, as if to tell me: *Mama, you are not alone.*

And so I built small altars of presence. Daily walks along the Amstel, even in the rain, pushing the kinderwagen[§]. Brewing tea in a cheap pot from Toko Dun Yong. Meeting Tatyana every Tuesday in Vondelpark to swap stories of sleepless nights. Reading *Nijntje*[#] to baby Milly, letting foreign syllables turn into lullabies.

---

* *Du'a* — a personal prayer in Islam, a whispered conversation with God in one's own words.

† *Surau* — the small prayer houses woven into Malaysian life, tucked into neighbourhoods, schools, and marketplaces, offering pause and prayer.

‡ *Zandbak* — Dutch for sandbox, a staple of nearly every playground where toddlers spend hours digging, building, and delighting.

§ *Kinderwagen* — Dutch for baby stroller or pram, pushed along bike paths and cobblestones, a familiar sight of daily life.

\# *Nijntje* (Miffy) — the beloved Dutch rabbit created by Dick Bruna in 1955, the gentle companion of many children's first stories.

Each ritual whispered: here too, you belong.

Presence was the only ground I had. Bureaucracy, weather, language — all kept shifting. The most radical thing I could do was to stop waiting for familiarity, and to claim belonging in the ordinary.

As the Dutch like to say, *"Doe maar gewoon, dan doe je al gek genoeg"* — just act normal, that's already crazy enough. In the small, steady rituals of daily life, I found the extraordinary gift of presence.

Beautiful Fractures

In Japan there is an art called *kintsugi** — golden joinery. When a bowl breaks, it is not discarded. The cracks are traced with lacquer mixed with gold, the fracture becoming the most luminous part of the vessel.

Migration does this to a life. Careers splinter. Friendships scatter. Identities fracture. You are tempted to hide the seams, to appear whole. But if you let truth and tenderness be the gold, the very lines of breaking begin to shine.

Years ago, I created a self-portrait: a broken woman, stitched together, fragile and fierce. I still find it beautiful. It felt honest, almost holy, to see my own face in pieces and yet holding together with unexpected grace. For a time I considered it as the cover of this book. But some found it disturbing. Their unease reminded me what I already knew: brokenness is beautiful to me, but not everyone can look directly at it.

So I set the portrait aside. Not because I doubt its beauty, but because I want these pages to be opened by hands that may not yet know how to love fracture as I do.

Still, the image lives with me. It reminds me that my inner

* *Kintsugi* (金継ぎ) — the Japanese art of repairing broken pottery with lacquer mixed with gold. Born in the 15th century, it transforms fracture into beauty, making the object more precious for having been broken.

scars are not something to disguise. They are part of the architecture of becoming. Proof that survival and beauty can coexist.

The breaks do not erase us. They inscribe us.

In Zen, even the brushstroke that bleeds beyond the line is part of the painting. In the same way, what cracked in me did not end the story. It traced the line that made it unmistakably mine.

Safe Enough to Stay

Letting go often sounds like a choice, but in truth it is a slow recalibration. The body, like the mind, clings to what it once knew.

Even when you have said yes to a new place, a new rhythm, a new version of yourself, your nervous system still scans for the landmarks it once called safety. This is not weakness. This is wiring.

The vagus nerve, a quiet thread from brainstem to belly, is always listening for cues. It asks: *Am I okay here? Can I soften? Can I stay?*

Back home, you knew what safe felt like. It lived in the sounds and smells, in the warmth of familiar glances, in the casual *"lah"* or *"a'ah"* that carried whole worlds of meaning.

In newness, everything is foreign. Your body does not understand why it jolts when it hears *"Lekker weer, hoor!"* * The amygdala flares. Cortisol rises. You breathe deeper without even realising it.

That is why small rituals matter. The cup of rooibos tea before bed. The path past the bent tree in Vondelpark. The baby group where you always choose the same chair by the window.

Even if no one else notices, these are not just routines. They are neural anchors. Each one tells your system: *You are okay now. You can root here.*

---

* *"Lekker weer, hoor!"* — literally "Lovely weather, isn't it!" For the Dutch, a phrase of delight when the sun appears after many grey days. A common greeting, shared joy in fleeting light.

Even if you do not belong yet, you are safe enough to stay.

Over time, this becomes your inner scaffolding. Not because life gets simpler, but because your body learns to trust its own intelligence again.

And that, truly, is letting go. Not forgetting the old place. Not pretending this one feels like home. But building a small corner of calm in the in-between.

You learn to trust yourself in small ways first. You take the tram without triple-checking the map. You stumble through the throaty syllables of a new language. You ask questions without apology. You notice which street feels kind, which neighbourhood feels safe.

And slowly, you remember what was always true: your body knows before your mind does. So you listen. You soften. You trust.

And in the end, it is these small anchors that whisper the quiet truth of the in-between: *You are safe enough to stay.*

Wu Wei (Allowing, Flowing)

The Taoists call it *wu wei**— effortless action, moving with the current instead of against it. Not passivity, but precision.

In migration, wu wei might look like this: learning a language slowly, without shame. Planting three friendships deeply instead of scattering thirty. Letting silence soften before you expect belonging.

Javanese wisdom echoes it: *alon-alon asal kelakon*† — slowly, as long as it is done. Steady progress carries more grace than frantic striving.

I did not grow up with *wu wei*. My childhood was filled with

* *Wu wei* (無為) — an ancient Taoist principle meaning "effortless action." Not passivity, but living in tune with the flow of life, as described in the *Tao Te Ching*.

† *Alon-alon asal kelakon* — Javanese saying: "Slowly, as long as it is done." A reminder that steady progress is more enduring than haste.

rules, not flow. There were paths already paved, expectations already set.

I only began to embrace *wu wei* when life left me no map. When Isabel was diagnosed with her rare condition, there were no instructions to follow. I was forced into the current. For the first time, the only way forward was surrender — to move with what was happening rather than against it.

That season taught me that acceptance is not resignation. It is the beginning of peace.

Wu wei became a way to belong to myself again. To let identity grow with life's rhythm, to avoid fracturing myself by forcing what could not be forced.

It is courage in another form. The courage to dance with life instead of battling it. The courage to trust that, even without pushing, we are already enough.

Migration is Spiritual

Self-trust is not loud. It does not announce itself. It is quiet. Earned. Built moment by moment.

It is choosing not to abandon yourself when things are not simple.

It is remembering that just because you feel unsure does not mean you are wrong.

It is holding space for fear, and for the not knowing.

And slowly, something roots. Not in the soil, but in you.

Not in permanence, but in presence.

Not in certainty, but in surrender.

You begin to understand: you are not lost.

You are shedding.

You are not broken. You are becoming.

You are not behind. You are moving at sacred, untamed time.

No one told you migration was a spiritual practice. But now you know. The gift is not only in arriving somewhere new. It is in meeting the version of yourself who knows how to stay soft in the unknown.

Some seasons do not bring dramatic plot twists. They are quiet. Grinding. Lonely. And sometimes it is in those very seasons that the deepest spiritual work unfolds.

For the Sufis*, to be a traveller is not only to cross landscapes, but to cross the terrain of the soul. To move through uncertainty until presence itself becomes home.

And this is what migration teaches us too: the in-between is not exile. It is the sacred ground of becoming.

Pace

Pace is never simple. In running, as in life, it rarely unfolds as you imagined.

I learned this during the Berlin Half Marathon. At the starting line it was zero degrees. Snowflakes clung to jackets and eyelashes. Yet I did not feel the cold. The air was alive with anticipation, hundreds of heartbeats waiting for the signal to begin.

By kilometre sixteen, my body ached. The Brandenburg Tor still felt impossibly far. My legs burned, my breath grew heavy, my feet pressed into the tarmac with stubborn rhythm. And in that ache, resilience whispered: *Keep going, but gently now.*

Long-distance running had already been teaching me this truth. Pace is not about speed, but about rhythm. It is knowing when to hold steady and when to release. It is listening to the body's signals — the quickened breath, the tightening calf, the quiet endurance in the lungs — and adjusting so you can last the distance.

Training for long runs is not about mastering the finish line, but trusting yourself kilometre by kilometre.

Motherhood in a foreign land often felt like kilometre sixteen.

* The Sufis — Islamic mystics who see travel not only as crossing land, but as a metaphor for the soul's journey through uncertainty toward divine presence.

All ache and no finish line in sight. My arms full, my identity shifting, my energy stretched thin.

Migration was the same. New languages. New systems. New maps. No clear markers of arrival. Only the rhythm of keeping on, step after step.

In both running and life, the terrain will change beneath your feet. You cannot control the weather. You cannot control the crowds. You cannot control what waits around the next bend.

What carries you forward is not control, but trust.

Trust that even a messy pace is still a pace.

Trust that slowing down is not failing.

Trust that gentleness is its own strength.

This is resilience. Not the loud kind that shouts of victory, but the quiet kind that lets you keep moving, one step at a time, even when the path feels uncertain.

The Resilience Equation

Resilience has been part of me for as long as I can remember — through migration, through reinvention, through the many times life asked me to begin again. But when Isabel was diagnosed, and I stepped away from the startups I had once poured myself into, I began to notice something unexpected: the two worlds echoed one another.

I had founded three startups. I knew the sleepless nights, the risk, the long road of building something from almost nothing. What no one tells you is that mothering a child with a rare condition can feel strangely similar. There is no manual. You learn as you go. You improvise, you adjust, you hold your breath for progress that comes more slowly than you hoped. And you celebrate the smallest wins, because you know they are not small at all — they are the foundation of everything that follows.

That parallel gave birth to the framework I later shared on the TEDx stage — a way of naming what I had lived through both in business and in motherhood:

$$\text{Resilience} = (\text{Time} \times \text{Mindset}) \wedge \text{Incremental Action}$$

Time: The world worships speed, but resilience asks for patience. A startup does not become a company overnight. A child does not unfold her potential on demand. Growth happens in seasons, in rhythms, often invisible until the moment it emerges.

Mindset: In both boardrooms and hospital rooms, humility is the only way forward. The Zen call it *shoshin*[*] — beginner's mind. You show up willing to learn, to be taught, to be reshaped. You stop pretending you know, and you let each challenge become a teacher.

Incremental Action: Both startups and children thrive on the small and the steady. A line of code improved, a pitch refined, a prototype tested. A new sound, a new gesture, a milestone reached. These tiny actions, repeated with devotion, compound into transformation.

This is resilience as I have come to know it: not the roar of triumph, but the rhythm of learning and beginning again. Not the pressure to be unbreakable, but the grace to remain human.

Resilience is the patience of time.

The humility of a learner.

The strength of small steps carried forward.

The Invisible Baggage

Many of us carry invisible baggage. It is packed with expectations and cultural scripts — the 'shoulds' that whisper: be grateful, be quicker, be stronger, be better, don't complain.

As a Southeast Asian, Malay, Muslim woman, my list was

---

[*] *Shoshin* (初心) — a Zen teaching often translated as "beginner's mind." It is the practice of meeting each moment with openness and curiosity, unburdened by assumption. A reminder that resilience is not rigid expertise, but the willingness to stay tender and awake to possibility.

long. The baggage stretched to hold unspoken demands until it was fit to burst.

Resilience, I learned, is not about carrying everything. It is about learning what to take out.

Letting go of narratives that no longer serve.

Letting go of shame for not being "on track."

Letting go of perfection in favour of presence.

I moved to Amsterdam to start a family. That choice rerouted the entire arc of my life. And when the marriage later ended, it wasn't aloneness that unsettled me. It was a deeper ache: the shame that I had failed — at forever, at the image, at the idea of the life I had promised myself. And threaded through it all was guilt. Two households. A child between them. The old questions: *Could you have tried harder? Stayed longer?*

But guilt isn't always wisdom. Sometimes it is conditioning wearing a moral tone.

So I began to unpack my baggage.

I let go of the idea that leaving meant I was broken.

I let go of staying for optics.

I let go of the compulsive comparison to women doing it "right."

I let go of the shame of not having a neat ending.

My life was never meant to be a theatre, nor an Instagram show.

In its place, I made room for truth: I felt lighter. I was never meant to shrink to keep something intact. A mother living in integrity is more powerful than a woman performing perfection.

Now, when the old weight tries to return, I pause. I remind myself: I did not fail. I evolved.

Letting go does not mean losing.

It means lightening the load.

Choosing new baggage. Simpler. Just enough for the road ahead.

And still, I wonder: for women like me, will the load always be heavy? In Malay we say, *Ringan sama dijinjing, berat sama* *dipikul* [*]— light loads we carry together; heavy burdens we shoulder together.

Yes, others can help lift. But no one else can live inside your skin. No one else can build the house within.

Companionship lightens the road; the architecture of your becoming remains yours. The inner house is not built by consensus, but by silent choices when no one is watching — what you keep, what you release, and how you carry what cannot be set down.

We walk together, but each of us must open our own baggage and turn the weight of expectation into the shelter of self.

Space for Fortuna

Fortes fortuna adiuvat. Fortune favours the open heart.

When you put down the invisible backpack, you do more than lighten your shoulders. You create space—space for new relationships, new values, new dreams you didn't know were allowed.

Perhaps it was Fortuna [†] who arranged for David and me to stand across from one another at the CASBAA Opening Party in Hong Kong—rooftop pool, humid air, France 24 banners, Tsim Sha Tsui glittering like a promise.

He walked over and handed me a business card as if it were the most ordinary thing. "Nina Aziz in Amsterdam... are you Indonesian?" he asked. I smiled at the map he guessed for me and

[*] The Malay saying *"Ringan sama dijinjing, berat sama dipikul"* — "light loads we carry together, heavy burdens we shoulder together" — is a reminder of solidarity. It honours the truth that companionship can ease what we carry, yet also acknowledges the sacred work that no one else can do for us: the inner labour of becoming ourselves.

[†] *Fortuna* — Roman goddess of chance (akin to the Greek Tyche), often pictured with a wheel to remind us how quickly fortune can turn. In these pages, she is less fate than permission—the space that opens when we set down the weight and make room for grace.

read his card back: "David Justin in New York... are you American?" We laughed softly at our polite misplacements. Not particularly romantic. But real.

I wasn't searching. I was making room—on my calendar, in my body, even in the small vacancy on my ring finger. And in that not-seeking, something gentle found us. Not a movie swell. A recognition. An ease.

What made it possible wasn't only timing. It was the clearing each of us had already carved—not to fill gaps, not to fix one another, but to share something already whole.

Two years later he left New York and moved to Amsterdam to join me and Camilla. He arrived on my birthday with two hundred boxes, calm confidence, and a small blue box carrying his lifetime promise—the same lopsided grin.

Letting go had made room. Not just for love, but for a love that didn't require performance.

Presence, not possession. Two people who knew who they were, choosing to grow together.

Home is not always a place or a role. Sometimes it is a person who meets you exactly where you are and is unafraid to build something beautiful beside you.

And slowly, listening to my intuition, a new confidence took root—the kind that says: *I may not know what comes next, but I trust who I am becoming.*

Perhaps that is Fortuna's gift: not merely the meeting, but the reminder that chance favours the heart that dares to make space.

The Shelter

This is where the idea of a home within deepens—not in the glitter of reinvention or the drama of departure, but in the ordinary, sacred work of showing up.

Showing up to your life. To your mess. To your joy.

When you learn to hold yourself with compassion, to stretch

without breaking, to ask for help and mean it, you are not only building resilience.

You are building shelter. Not on land, but in soul.

A shelter that does not depend on geography.

A shelter that moves with you. A soothing, steady refuge you can always return to.

Perhaps this is Fortuna's final kindness: chance may open the door, but your tenderness turns it into belonging.

Part 2: THE BECOMING

The Reinvention
The Motherhood
The Self-definition

Chapter 5

Not from Scratch

Start Where You Are

Not all reinvention arrives with a plan. Sometimes it begins with a gift you haven't expected.

And that is where reinvention begins.

Not because you are broken.

Not because you failed.

People call it "starting over." But we never begin from nothing. We begin from what survived. From the wisdom etched into us. From the scars that taught us how to mend.

We begin with a nervous system that has already weathered storms, with an inner compass that speaks more clearly than before.

When I moved to Amsterdam, it was not the path I had envisaged. I had been preparing to return to Asia for a career opportunity that looked like everything I had dreamed of. Instead, life handed me something entirely different — the gift of becoming a mother and I wanted to embrace what arrived, and to trust that joy and strength could grow even in uncertain soil. That choice — tender, risky, and brave in its own way — became the seed of everything that has unfolded into my life today.

Ambition and career had always been part of my foundation. I grew up watching my mother and my aunties work, and from an early age I understood resourcefulness and independence as the shape of life. I looked after my younger brother, learned to rely on myself, and carried that model into adulthood.

So when I chose to build my life in Europe, far from family, I was not surprised to be mothering without a close role model nearby. It was not new. What was new was the chance to shape motherhood differently — to draw from memory and instinct, but also to choose which patterns to keep and which ones to release. That absence was not only a challenge, but also a kind of freedom.

I remember pushing Camilla's pram along the Amstel, the river covered by morning fog outside the place we once lived. My feet moved steadily over the cobblestones, and in that rhythm I was washed with gratitude. This was not the life I had planned, but somehow it felt like the one I was meant to live. I knew I wanted to be a good, loving mother to her — even if I had no idea how. All I knew was that I would learn on the job, and I would do my ultimate best. And in that simple knowing, something in me softened: perhaps this heartfelt intention was enough to begin with.

Much of who we are is written early. Our brains wire themselves through observation, repeating the patterns of those who raised us*. We inherit their resilience, their reflexes, their ways of surviving the world. And yet here lies the paradox: I am my mother, but I do not want to be her. Her story is the foundation, but not the home I wish to build. I honour her strength, but I long for a different shape of life.

Perhaps you know this feeling too — to look in the mirror and see your parent's face flicker back at you, to hear their voice echo

* Early childhood is when the brain is most malleable. Neural pathways form rapidly through what we observe, imitate, and repeat. Psychologists call this "model learning" — the patterns of resilience, fear, and response laid down in these years become the scaffolding on which later choices are built.

in your own words, and still feel the urgency to choose differently. We inherit their blueprint, but we do not want to inhabit it entirely.

It is like receiving a house already built: some walls stand strong, others confine. And so we spend our lives deciding which walls to keep, which to tear down, and where to add new windows so more light can enter.

This resistance is not rejection. It is evolution. It is love stretching into something new. Awareness interrupting programming. Neuroplasticity carving fresh pathways where old ones would have led us. One small decision at a time, the story bends.

So while I did not have a detailed plan, I did have a compass. A vision of the kind of mother I wanted to be, and the kind of life I could not bear to inhabit. I knew I wanted career and ambition to remain part of my story, but I also knew I wanted motherhood to feel expansive, not constricting. That tension became my guide.

Reinvention came not as certainty, but as self-determination. A promise to build differently.

Not with a map, but with memory and longing, with desire and refusal, with the gentle insistence that life could be more than inherited scripts.

Reinvention, for me, is not a grand entrance. It is the moment I recognise myself again, in a new situation. It is stepping, at last, beyond the threshold — into the reception of my home within — because reinvention always begins by starting where you are.

Mirrors of Change

What no one tells you about moving away is that culture shock is not only about arrival. It is about staying long enough to lose small pieces of yourself — and then missing them in sharp, unexpected ways. It is saying something kind and watching it land as weakness. It is craving *sambal* while being served *salade de riz** by my French *belle maman*†, smiling politely while my tongue longs for fire.

I think back to a morning in Kuala Lumpur, standing at a business workshop. I told a story with a funny line, expecting the familiar release of laughter. Instead: silence. Blank stares. Tight, polite smiles. The punchline dissolved in the air, untranslatable. It was not offensive. It simply did not belong. Heat crawled up my spine, not from embarrassment but from the cold recognition that my social currency had expired.

What had once been fluency was now foreign. I realised I did not only need to learn a new language. I needed to relearn my rhythm. This is the quiet kind of culture shock. Not the dramatic arrival at a new airport, but the small ruptures that creep in quietly. It is the sudden ache on your birthday when familiar voices cannot gather around your table. It is the sharpness of a question in the visa office, reducing your life to paperwork.

It is the casual query, "When are you going home?" And you hear your own thought: "Wait a minute, I am home." Not the kind they mean. Not a flag, not a residence permit, not a childhood address. Just here. In your skin. In the decision to keep showing up, even when the room no longer recognises you. In the quiet resistance to invisibility.

Science tells us that nothing in life stands still. Every atom is in motion, colliding, becoming. Every cell is shedding, repairing, renewing. By the time you finish reading this page, millions of your cells will have died and been replaced. Biology itself is a lesson in impermanence. Survival depends on adaptation — not on clinging to what was, but on reshaping into what can be.

---

* *Salade de riz*: a cold rice salad of tuna, vegetables, and mayonnaise, a summer staple in many French households, light and unassuming in its quiet comfort.

† *Belle maman*: the French way of saying "mother-in-law," literally "beautiful mother," softening kinship into tenderness.

The natural world carries the same truth. A bird* no bigger than a hand flies from Arctic Circle to Antarctic ice and back each year, chasing light. Another crosses the Pacific without rest, spanning oceans in a single stretch of faith†. Trees surrender their leaves each autumn, not as failure but as wisdom — conserving what they cannot keep, so they may rise again in spring‡.

Resilience is the same. It is not born from clutching at what once worked. It is born from noticing, adjusting, moving with the rhythm of change. Each silence we meet, each smile that falters, each question that unsettles — all are mirrors, showing us not only who we are, but who we are becoming.

What the world reflects back to us may not always be gentle, but it is always instructive. And the more we allow ourselves to evolve alongside it, the more resilient we become — finding home not in permanence, but in the endless capacity to keep becoming.

Identity Is Neural

We often think of growth as an attitude. Just mindset. Just grit. But science shows us it is more than that. Growth is not only mental. It is biological. The brain is built first for survival, not for expansion. It clings to the known, even when the familiar is no longer true, even when it hurts us.

Yet hidden in this design is a gift: the brain is also plastic. It can adapt. It can rewire. It wants to keep us alive, but it is also capable of helping us evolve.

Every time you say yes to something real, even when it terrifies you, you are reshaping your inner architecture. This is why

* The Arctic tern makes the longest migration of any bird — over 70,000 kilometres each year between the poles, a lifetime equal to three journeys to the moon.

† The bar-tailed godwit can cross the Pacific in a single flight of more than 11,000 kilometres, nine days without pause.

‡ Deciduous trees shed leaves in autumn to conserve strength, storing energy for the renewal of spring — a reminder that resilience often looks like release before growth.

change leaves us so tired. You are not only making decisions — you are growing new pathways, asking your neurons to reach for one another in patterns they have never held before.

I know this in my own bones. Throughout my life, relationships with men have always been complicated terrain. I could love deeply, but when things grew serious, I would often retreat. I thought I was not made for permanence, even though I was always a monogamist at heart.

So when David proposed, I was frightened — I hadn't seen it coming, and part of me wanted to run away out of habit. But something in me shifted. I said yes, and with time, that yes grew into a home and a partnership more beautiful than I ever thought I could sustain.

I carried the same fear when I said yes to my TEDx talk. I worried about whether I could deliver something worthy. Yet once again, stepping into that yes rewired me — leaving me stronger, steadier, and more alive.

Reinvention is not only about taking action. It is about reassembly. It is emotional, spiritual, and cellular. Your very wiring is participating in your becoming.

Think of it like a house. At first it looks solid, familiar. The walls hold stories, the windows frame a view you know by heart. But if you stay long enough, you notice the cracks in the plaster, the pipes that no longer run clean, the doors that no longer close properly. Renovation is not a choice if you want the house to stand. So you strip back, rewire, replace beams, open new windows. You do not lose the house. You rebuild it from the inside out.

Identity works in the same way. And here is the paradox: whatever you believe you are, you are right. Psychology calls it the self-fulfilling prophecy: when we expect failure, we shrink from opportunities; when we expect possibility, we step into it.

Neuroscience confirms it: thoughts of hope release dopamine, giving us motivation to act, while beliefs of helplessness can shut down the circuits of initiative. The stories we repeat inside ourselves are not abstract. They sculpt our biology.

Ancient wisdom knew this long before science named it. The Greeks told of warriors who won because they trusted the gods were with them, and of others undone by doubt before the battle even began. In the *Bhagavad Gita**, Arjuna falters in despair until Krishna reminds him that to trust his *dharma*†, his purpose, is the first step toward courage. In Islamic teaching, the Prophet Muhammad said, "Trust in God, but tie your camel" — a reminder that belief fuels action rather than replacing it. Across ages and cultures, the message is the same: conviction shapes destiny.

History, too, is full of leaders who rose on the strength of belief and crumbled when it deserted them. Empires expanded and collapsed on the stories people told themselves about who they were and what they could endure.

Belief, then, is not decoration. It is blueprint. It tells your neurons how to connect, your body how to prepare, your spirit how to rise. This is why resilience is not only endurance but imagination. It begins in the unseen choices — the inner blueprints we sketch behind the doors of our heart, when no one is looking.

Change your blueprint, and the house within begins to shift. Slowly, imperceptibly at first, then unmistakably, you become a different home for yourself.

Your home within is not static. It is neuro-plastic.

It is responsive. It is alive.

---

* The *Bhagavad Gita* ("Song of God"), part of the Indian epic *Mahabharata*, is framed as a dialogue between the warrior Arjuna and Krishna. It has long been read as a meditation on duty, courage, and the purpose that steadies the soul in times of despair.

† *Dharma* in Hindu thought is the principle of sacred duty and right action — the path that aligns a person's life with truth and deeper purpose.

Time as a Currency

In migration, time feels different. Ordinary tasks take longer. A doctor's form in another language. A train that runs on rules you do not yet know. A letter from the tax office that sits unopened on the counter for weeks.

Time disappears in the smallest things. Layer ambition, study, relationships, or caregiving into the mix, and the hours contract further. I often felt as if I were living under two clocks: one for my inner life, one for my outer obligations. Both always out of sync. The guilt was constant. The sense of scarcity louder than any success.

What I learned from this inner conundrum is that time is not only about hours. It is about presence. Ten minutes of real attention to someone I love was worth more than a distracted afternoon. One mindful hour of work produced more than three anxious ones. Time cannot be stretched. But it can be savoured.

Modern life has made time a commodity — something to be bought, sold, scheduled, optimised. Yet physics reminds us that time is not absolute at all. Einstein showed us that time bends with speed and gravity*. Quantum physics suggests it may ripple and overlap, rather than march in a straight line. What feels like a minute in one frame of reference can be an eternity in another.

For the migrant, time becomes even more layered. You live with the clock of your new country, but also with the invisible time zone of the place you left. You may be drinking morning coffee while your family across the ocean prepares to sleep. You may feel older or younger than your peers, depending on how quickly you adapted.

Migration is not only about crossing borders, but about learning to inhabit multiple clocks at once.

Ancient traditions have always known that time is more than a

* Einstein showed that time is not fixed but bends with speed and gravity — even physics agrees it is fluid.

clock — in Hindu thought, *kāla* unfolds in vast cycles of ages, while in Buddhism, each breath reminds us the only real time is the present. The Greeks distinguished between *chronos*, measured and linear, and *kairos*, the sacred moment. In Islam, time is sanctified as *waqt*, the appointed hour of prayer. And in many Indigenous traditions, time is a circle, where ancestors and descendants are present at once.

Modern psychology now echoes this ancient wisdom. Studies show that those who value time over money tend to report greater happiness, stronger relationships, and a deeper sense of meaning*. Scarcity of money can be overcome, but scarcity of time cannot. Time is the only currency that, once spent, can never be earned back.

Mathematics reminds us of this with brutal clarity. A life of eighty years is 29,200 days, or about 700,000 hours. Subtract sleep, and you are left with closer to 400,000 waking hours. Every choice is made within this finite frame. To exchange hours only for money without meaning is to miscalculate the true equation of value.

This is why, when I stood on the TEDx stage, I framed resilience as an equation:

Resilience = (Time × Mindset) ^ Incremental Action

At first glance it looks like numbers, but to me it was a truth written in symbols. Time matters because it sets the scale of growth — it is the multiplier. A brilliant mindset or bold action cannot become resilience if rushed. Like compound interest, presence gathers power only when it is given room to accumulate.

Resilience is slow mathematics. It is the steady layering of choices, the quiet compounding of breath, thought, and step, across days, months, years.

Proverbs across cultures have always known this. The

* Research in psychology suggests that choosing time over money is linked with greater happiness and meaning (Hershfield et al., 2016).

Japanese remind us, *Ishi no ue ni mo san nen** — even a cold stone will grow warm if you sit on it long enough. The Malaysians say, *Sedikit-sedikit, lama-lama jadi bukit* †— little by little, over time, a hill becomes a mountain.

Wisdom in every tongue agrees: resilience is not instant. It is harvested in time. And perhaps the deepest gift we can offer ourselves, especially when life is stretched across borders and change, is to take the time we need to arrive fully in our own skin.

Time is not just a clock ticking. It is the enduring mason of the self, always becoming.

A Jazz Ensemble

There is a grief no one warns you about: the grief of loosening your grip on the selves that once kept you safe. Because when you have lived across borders and changes, there was never just one.

There was the self in Malaysia, who grew up with the rhythm of the call to prayer, family rituals, and the heat of *sambal* on her tongue, who learned early how to move with grace inside the weave of tradition. The self in England, who learned to speak in codes, to soften her edges, to hold her fork with the tines down and pile the food onto the back, in polite company‡. The self in Germany, who absorbed order and efficiency, who came to revere a timetable as if it were scripture. The self in the Netherlands, who pedalled through wind and rain, discovering that the secret to being special was to be completely *normaal*§. And the self in France, who studied the language of elegance and could name her

* Japanese proverb: "Sit on a stone for three years." Patience softens hardship and allows change to come.

† Malaysian proverb: "Little by little, a hill becomes a mountain." Small acts, carried by time, become transformation.

‡ In Britain, etiquette still carries echoes of history: forks in the left hand, tines down, knives nudging food onto the back — a ritual of refinement that endures.

§ The Dutch saying *doe normaal* ("just act normal") reflects a culture that values modesty and pragmatism, where ordinariness itself is a virtue.

camembert from her *comté* — but also learned that "camembert" might just mean *"shut your mouth."

Each self adjusted, adapted, made herself acceptable. Each carried her own bundle of strategies, her own keys for survival. They taught me how to read a room, when to stay quiet, how to make myself small enough to belong. For years, they worked like guardians. And I would not be here without them.

But sometimes the world asks you to choose. My mother, with love and exasperation, complains that I am "too Western." In the West, I am reminded I am not Western enough. In those moments, I feel as if I am standing in front of an orchestra pit with too many instruments in my hands, unsure which one I am allowed to play. Pick one, and I betray the others. Leave them all, and there is only silence.

It was only years later, in hypnotherapy with Thevi — my extraordinary hypnotherapist who beams into my living room on Zoom — that I began to see them differently. She taught me that these selves are not fractured identities but musicians in the same band. They do not need to be discarded. They need to tune to one another.

The Malaysian self bringing fire, faith, and rootedness. The English self offering codes of belonging. The German self keeping a steady beat of order. The Dutch self pedalling stamina into the rhythm. The French self slipping in a riff of beauty, language, and wit. When I let them play together instead of competing, I realised they were not holding me back at all. They were composing something larger.

Not a broken record, but jazz — a living improvisation where discord folds back into harmony, and no single note is wasted†.

Psychology tells us the self is not singular but layered, shifting

* In France, to be told to "close your camembert box" is a playful way of saying "enough talking." Even cheese becomes idiom.

† Jazz, born in New Orleans, turned rhythm and discord into freedom. At its heart is improvisation — a reminder that contradictions can create harmony.

with context. Neuroscience adds that the brain itself is a mosaic of pathways, strengthened by both repetition and novelty. Like jazz, it thrives on structure and freedom, on rhythm and surprise. Integration is the real art.

So I gather all of my selves now, not with shame or rejection, but with reverence. They are not fractures but foundations. Each brings its own rhythm, its own riff, its own story of survival. Sometimes one leads, sometimes another improvises, sometimes they clash before finding their way back to harmony. And when they play together, it is not noise but a living, breathing chorus — improvisational, surprising, unmistakably mine.

This is the sound of my belonging: not a single instrument, but an ensemble. A music that fills the home within, turning every room into part of the song.

El Duende en Contra Tiempo

Balance is one of the great illusions we are sold in the modern world. There is an entire economy around it now, almost as lucrative as Ozempic. We are told we can give everything to those we love and still remain fully ourselves. We are told we can excel in our work and never miss a moment at home. No one explains how.

When I became a mother, I loved my daughters fiercely, yet I grieved the parts of me that seemed to vanish in their shadow. But even before motherhood, as an entrepreneur scaling businesses across continents, I knew the myth well. In one world, I was in boardrooms, closing deals and speaking on stages. In another, I was at home, invisible to the world but indispensable in the smallest, most ordinary ways. Holding both identities in one body often felt like tearing.

Some days, the entrepreneur envied the simplicity of home. Some days, the caregiver longed for the recognition of the stage. Both selves tugged at me, asking to be chosen. But balance, I came to learn, is not about choosing. Selfhood and care are not enemies; they are roots of the same tree. One grounds you, the other stretches you. Balance is not dividing yourself into perfect halves. It is letting both roots drink.

Flamenco taught me this long before I could name it. For years, before I fell pregnant with Camilla, I danced. I spent long stretches of time in Sevilla at Taller de Flamenco, giving my summers to rhythm. Mornings began with *compás*[*], then footwork drills, then choreography. Afternoons were for siesta, evenings for friends in *Triana*[†]. We gathered on rooftops with guitars and *cajón*[‡], singing into the night, creating our own *tablaos*[§] under the stars. That was time for self — carved out with sweat, music, and joy.

What I loved most was *contra tiempo*: the art of striking against the expected beat. Flamenco lives in that tension — the off-beat that disrupts yet completes the music. It is not balance in the neat sense of symmetry, but a balance born of dissonance, of push and pull. Motherhood and selfhood, too, are *contra tiempo*[#]. They tug against each other, they refuse to align neatly, yet together they create the rhythm of a larger song.

When I stopped fighting their opposition, I noticed their dialogue. The entrepreneur carried confidence into the playground, teaching courage in unfamiliar spaces. The caregiver softened the businesswoman's edges, reminding her that tenderness belongs in boardrooms too. Together they gave me a life far messier and more demanding than I expected — but also far richer.

---

* *Compás* — The rhythmic cycle at the heart of flamenco; its living heartbeat. To lose the *compás* is to lose the dance itself.

† *Triana* — A historic neighbourhood of Seville, long considered the cradle of flamenco, where courtyards, taverns, and workshops gave rise to its soul.

‡ *Cajón* — A wooden box-shaped drum played by hand, now central to modern flamenco rhythm.

§ *Tablao* — An intimate flamenco stage, often in cafés or bars, where performers and audience breathe as one.

\# *Contra tiempo* — Striking against the expected beat. The syncopation that creates tension and surprise, embodying flamenco's essence: discipline and freedom, tradition and rebellion.

In flamenco they say, *"El duende no se busca, te encuentra"* — the spirit does not wait to be chased; it finds you. I think of that when I consider the two clocks I live by. They are not separate lives to choose between, but rhythms that sometimes clash, sometimes entwine, always carrying me forward.

Balance, I realised, is not a tightrope. It is *compás* — the deep pulse that holds flamenco steady, surprising and alive. Sometimes one voice is louder, sometimes the other, yet both belong to the same song.

The lesson was never in balance but in *el duende en contra tiempo* — the spirit that arrives in the off-beat, the beauty born from tension, the magic that only appears when life dares to dance outside the expected rhythm.

The Red Dot

Rebuilding is an inside job. You rebuild not with grand declarations, but with small, holy decisions. You wear what feels like you. You speak even when your voice shakes. You stay silent when silence itself carries power. You stop apologising for your bigness, your softness, your ambition. You do you.

You do not need to be new.

You need to be true.

You need to own your presence without shrinking to fit the room.

When I spoke at TEDx Coolhaven Women, I walked on stage wearing a white professional shirt and a Malay sarong. Bright, unapologetic, lime green. The kind of colour that refuses invisibility.

It was not just any sarong. It was *batik*[*] — a modern design by

---

[*] *Batik* is a traditional textile of the Malay world, created through a wax-resist dyeing technique. Its motifs often draw from nature — flowers, leaves, waves, constellations — carrying the rhythm of balance and harmony. Dutch traders once carried the technique to West Africa, where it blossomed into vibrant wax prints, showing how cloth, like people, migrates and reinvents itself.

Lisette Scheers of Nala, one of my favourite Malaysian brands. *Batik*, like me, has travelled across seas and empires, yet always carries the memory of its first soil. Lisette herself has lived the life I have lived in reverse: Dutch raised in Malaysia, weaving East and West into her craft. Wearing her cloth felt like wearing my own truth — that I, too, carry cultures, languages, and landscapes within me, not as contradictions but as companions.

To stand on 'The Red Dot'* wrapped in her batik was to stand inside that dialogue: a Dutch woman who found her home in Kuala Lumpur, a Malaysian woman who built hers in Amsterdam. Two lives, a fabric of shared belonging.

That day, I felt aligned. Not only in what I wore, but in who I was.

Alignment matters. Spiritual traditions tell us that when inner life and outer action match, a deeper flow appears. In yoga, it is union. In Sufism, it is *tawhid*†, the oneness of being. Cognitive science echoes the same truth: when values and behaviour align, the brain releases the chemistry of authenticity. Misalignment, by contrast, sparks restlessness, stress, the gnawing ache of dissonance.

This is why alignment is not vanity.

It is vitality.

It is the courage to show up without disguise, to let your history, your values, your becoming, be visible in the choices you make.

Cloth can carry that truth. When I wrapped myself in batik on that stage, I was not only wearing design. I was carrying ancestry, craft, and continuity. Cloth has the power to soften boundaries, to weave East and West into harmony, to hold tradition and reinvention at once.

---

* The "red dot" is the circular carpet on every TED stage. It has become a symbol of presence — the idea that one person, rooted in that circle, can share an idea powerful enough to reach the world.

† In Islamic teaching, *tawhid* is the principle of oneness — God without partner or division, and life as interconnected through that unity.

So can colour. That day I wore lime green, a shade that does not whisper but sings. Green is the colour of renewal, of landscapes after rain. In Islam it holds sacred weight, a colour of paradise and peace. To wear lime green on that stage was to carry both my heritage and my hope, to stand alive, unhidden, whole.

And then I remembered a little girl who once loved a pencil case with a red double-decker bus printed on it. How miraculous that something so ordinary could hold such prophecy. A pencil case became a compass. A red bus became a symbol of self-belief. And years later, on that red dot, I realised she had been leading me here all along.

I wasn't trying to be bold. I was trying to be honest. I was trying to honour the little girl who had once dared to dream.

I stood on the red dot with her — and with every self I had ever been: the Malaysian, the English, the German, the Dutch, the French. It felt as though my entire jazz ensemble had arrived, each instrument tuning into harmony, no longer competing but playing together.

And in that moment, I felt a surge of gratitude for all the twists and turns that had led me to that circle. The stage itself seemed to widen, as if it, too, knew what it meant to carry a child's dream inside a grown woman's voice.

Enough-ness

You are not here to be your parents' or ancestors' do-over at life. You are a vessel of gold-lined fault lines, repaired with tenderness.

Perhaps the invitation was always to dance with the seasons of giving and the seasons of rest, to tango with the times of noise and the times of silence.

Migration has no manual, motherhood no blueprint, life no guarantees.

But in rhythm we can find not the rigid symmetry of perfection, but the sway that lets us bend without breaking. The pulse that holds us steady through both chaos and calm.

The kind of flow Eminem rapped about, losing yourself so completely in the moment that it rewrites your story.

The kind of truth Lady Gaga sang of, that you were "Born this Way," whole from the beginning, never needing reinvention to be worthy.

And the kind of revelation cinema gave us in **Everything Everywhere All At Once*, led by Michelle Yeoh — a fellow Malaysian who stood on the world's biggest stage and reminded us that even in infinite universes the greatest power lies not in becoming extraordinary, but in honouring the ordinary you have always been.

Rhythm is not about choosing sides. It is about letting life keep time with itself. It is about building a home within that does not demand symmetry, only honesty.

And that is enough. This is what it means to belong — to sway, to stay, to be. Enough-ness is not something you chase. It is something you come home to.

---

* *Everything Everywhere All At Once* (2022), directed by Daniel Kwan and Daniel Scheinert, became the first film with an all-Asian cast to sweep the Academy Awards, winning seven Oscars including Best Picture. Michelle Yeoh, born in Malaysia, made history as the first Asian woman to win the Academy Award for Best Actress. The film has been praised for blending absurdist comedy, science fiction, and tender family drama, while carrying a universal message: that even in infinite universes, the greatest power lies in honouring the ordinary love and life you already have.

Chapter 6

Love in Other Worlds

It Was Never Meant to Be

When we are young, we believe love can be engineered. That if we work hard enough, compromise deeply enough, insist tenderly enough, we can bend the laws of life to our will. We imagine ourselves authors of destiny, foolishly certain that passion alone can rewrite what centuries of culture, family, and faith have inscribed in our bones.

But time and heartbreak reveal a quieter truth: life is not a script we direct, but a tide we learn to move with. As the Stoics reminded us, control is illusion. Marcus Aurelius wrote, "Accept the things to which fate binds you, and love the people with whom fate brings you together, but do so with all your heart." Love is not a conquest. It is a gift that arrives, often carrying the weight of histories far older than us.

Eastern wisdom echoes this surrender. In the Tao Te Ching, Lao Tzu teaches that water prevails not by force but by yielding, flowing around obstacles rather than against them. Love too must flow, and sometimes it must recede, not because it failed, but because the banks of our lives could not yet hold it.

My first great love was an English gentleman. I still remember the cadence of his voice, the melody of my name spoken in his accent, as if it had been waiting all along for those syllables.

He asked me once, with a simplicity that startled my twenty-three-year-old self: "Are you happy?" We had just stepped out of a Russian film in Knightsbridge. I remember the city lights, the way my chest tightened with both giddiness and awe.

He was cultured, kind, even able to fry a respectable *nasi goreng**, proof to me then that bridges could be built across culture through our food too.

For a while, it felt true. But love is not only about two hearts. It is about the unseen architecture around them: rituals, unspoken codes, ancestral echoes. Who speaks in silence. Who carries sacrifice. Who interprets faith.

We never even fully named the wound but religion pressed between us like an invisible wall. Expectations clung to us like shadows. He offered me his grandmother's ring and a hand in marriage but our love was not muscular enough to carry it forward.

It ended with thunder. The love remained, but its form could not.

And so we loved each other differently, from afar. Gently. Without blame. Because sometimes the deepest ache is not that love disappears, but that it cannot take root in the soil it finds.

Buddhism † teaches that clinging is the root of suffering;

---

* *Nasi goreng*, literally "fried rice," is one of the most beloved and adaptable dishes in the Malay Archipelago, spanning Malaysia, Indonesia, Singapore, Thailand, Vietnam and Brunei. More than just a way to repurpose leftover rice, it is a canvas for memory and identity. Every household and street stall has its own version, carrying the rhythms of daily life: a quick breakfast before school, a midnight snack after weddings, or the dish that welcomes you home from a journey.

† In Buddhist teaching, the Second Noble Truth describes how suffering (*dukkha*) arises from craving and clinging (*tanhā*). When we attach ourselves too tightly to people, outcomes, or ideals, we suffer the inevitable ache of impermanence.

perhaps that is why the gentlest act of love is release, honouring what was beautiful, even as we surrender what could never be.

What I learned was this: not all stories are meant to last, but all are meant to shape us.

Cross-cultural love often ends not for lack of tenderness, but for lack of a home wide enough to hold two entire histories. It was never meant to be, not because it wasn't real, but because its time and place could not contain it.

And still, it meant everything.

The Black Horse

Love returned in seasons, each one carrying a different accent, a different lesson. Catalan. Magyar. Dutch. They came not as trophies but as teachers, each offering me a mirror to the parts of myself I had not yet met.

In my twenties, I thought love could be managed by effort and compromise, as if devotion alone might override destiny. But love, like life, resists control.

The Greeks spoke of *Eros* as both gift and madness, and Rumi wrote that love is "the bridge between you and everything." I was still learning that not all bridges are meant to last. Some are simply passages to the next version of yourself.

The Catalan loved fiercely. Expressive, adoring, always reaching for my hand in the street. "Ninetta, t'estimo molt." I love you very much, little Nina ... His devotion was beautiful, and sometimes overwhelming. I had not yet found the words to say I needed space, that intimacy in my Malay heart often took private, gentler forms.

The Magyar was lavish. He poured out gifts and grandeur as if abundance alone could guarantee connection. He called it passion; I called it heavy. Malay humility longed for moderation more than spectacle.

The Dutchman was steady, practical, direct. Logistics were

his love language. He grounded me in reliability, but I missed the sense of being cherished.

These men were not failures. They were seasons. And woven into these seasons was another paradox I had to untangle.

Growing up in Malaysia, my darker skin* had marked me as less than. I was told, again and again, that beauty was fair, that my shade made me undesirable and 'ugly'.

When I was busy playing tennis under the tropical sun, boys would serenade"*Kuda Hitam*" †the Black Horse, mocking me for being dark-skinned. Even at home, there were moments when the prejudice seeped into love: my own mother, half-joking but echoing the weight of our culture, would say that because I was sporty, sweaty, and dark, no one would ever want to marry me.

I remember confiding in my late grandmother, Wan Jah. In her grounding and cavalier way, she told me: "*Sometimes when you are different, it is because you are blessed.*" Her words softened the sting, but the wound of colourism lingered.

Yet years later, in the West, the same features drew attention. Suddenly, my difference was not a flaw but a fascination. At the beginning it felt uncomfortably awkward when someone says they find me attractive. Some of it was genuine admiration, some of it the shallow curiosity of the 'exotic.'

In big cities, where cosmopolitan life is celebrated, mixed couples were almost fashionable, a symbol of global belonging. It

---

* Across much of Asia, fair or white skin has long been upheld as an ideal of beauty. While part of this preference predates colonialism — linked to class distinctions between agricultural labourers who worked under the sun and elites who stayed indoors — colonial encounters amplified and codified the bias. European presence in South and Southeast Asia reinforced the association of lightness with wealth, education, and power, embedding "fairness" into beauty standards, advertising, and even marriage expectations. The aftershocks of this colonial hierarchy linger today in skin-lightening industries, social perceptions, and the quiet but pervasive judgments passed on darker-skinned children.

† "*Kuda Hitam*" ("Black Horse") is a song popularized by the Indonesian singer Hetty Koes Endang. In my childhood, it became a teasing chant among boys to mock darker-skinned peers—a small song, but one that revealed how deeply colourism had seeped into daily life.

was disorienting to realise that what had once been used to wound me could, elsewhere, become a source of allure.

This too was a lesson, a mirror of how beauty is never inherent but always filtered through culture, power, and place. Each one left behind not only memories, but lessons. They showed me what resonated, what jarred, where my vulnerabilities lived. They revealed the invisible ways culture shapes intimacy, and the courage it takes to stay true to yourself when another's love asks you to bend.

Eastern thought reminded me that clinging breeds suffering, because everything changes. Taoism teaches that love, like water, flows where it can and recedes where it must. The Stoics*, too, urged acceptance of fate, trusting that life weaves patterns larger than our plans.

So I began to see these seasons not as losses, but as apprenticeships in love.

They taught me that compatibility is not control, but resonance. That real love is not about being completed, but about being revealed.

Tak Apa

In every culture, there are phrases that hold more than words. In my Malay world, one of them is *tak apa*† — "never mind," "it's okay." At first glance, it seems simple, even careless. But beneath it

* The Stoics taught that serenity comes from recognising what lies within our control — our thoughts, choices, and actions — and accepting with equanimity what does not. Epictetus reminded his students, "Some things are up to us and some are not," while Marcus Aurelius urged, "Accept the things to which fate binds you."

† A Malay phrase meaning "never mind" or "it's okay." It reflects cultural values of patience, adaptability, and social harmony. While sometimes seen as resignation, it is often used as a gesture of grace: to de-escalate conflict, to forgive mistakes, to keep moving without bitterness. It embodies a cultural ease that softens the pursuit of perfection.

lives a philosophy: a way of softening life, forgiving mistakes, loosening the grip on perfection.

Growing up, I heard *tak apa* everyday, on the streets, in kitchens, at school gates and family tables. It was how we smoothed over quarrels, how elders consoled us after failure, how neighbours let small grievances slide. To an outsider, it might look like complacency. To us, it was resilience — a survival rhythm that allowed life to go on without bitterness.

For years I lost touch with this ease, trading it for Western ideals of ambition, achievement, and certainty. But as I have grown older, I have found myself returning to *tak apa* as part of my architecture of self. It is not avoidance, but grace. Not passivity, but perspective.

For a long time, I thought love was about finding someone who fit neatly into the house of my life, as if they would simply move in and occupy the rooms already built. But love, I have learned, is an architect. It redraws the blueprint. It tears down walls, opens new windows, alters the foundations.

Every relationship left me with a question: Which part of myself did I lose in translation, and which part did I discover? Which pieces of my Malay inheritance did I long to preserve — humility, concealed spiritual devotion, the sacredness of ritual — and which did I need to release so that love could breathe?

Psychology tells us we cannot build forward if we abandon what lies beneath. Studies show that children who grow up knowing their family stories — not just the triumphs, but also the struggles — develop greater resilience and self-esteem*.

Migrants, too, flourish when they carry their roots into new lives rather than erasing them†. Roots are not anchors that weigh

---

* Cross-cultural psychology (Benet-Martínez & Haritatos, 2005) finds that migrants who integrate heritage with host culture report higher well-being than those who erase their roots.

† Research at Emory University by Marshall Duke and Robyn Fivush (1997–2010) showed that children who know their family history, including both successes and struggles, develop stronger resilience, identity, and self-esteem.

us down; they are the soil that steadies us. Without them, the architecture of the self risks becoming hollow, a façade without foundation. With them, we grow not in spite of where we came from, but because of it.

Love, too, is a builder. It reveals the scaffolding we no longer need, the staircases that lead nowhere, the rooms that have grown too small. It asks us to notice where the ceilings press down, and where we are invited to rise higher.

Across cultures, architecture has always carried wisdom about the self. In Japan, *ma* — the beauty of space and pause — reminds us that emptiness can hold meaning as deeply as form.

My own Malay phrase *tak apa* is another kind of architecture: a loosening of perfection, an ease that forgives both self and world. These teachings remind me that strength is found as much in what we release as in what we build.

Perhaps this is why I am drawn to simplicity now. To structures where beauty lives in clarity rather than excess. I think of Doug Aitken's *Mirage*, a mirrored house in the California desert that vanishes into its surroundings. Its lesson is profound: sometimes beauty lies not in addition, but in blending with what already is.

So what is love, if not a living blueprint?

It is not the polished building, complete and perfect. It is the dialogue between structure and change. The courage to reimagine the house of the self whenever a new season arrives.

I used to believe the measure of love was permanence. Now I see it differently: the true measure of love is what it builds in you. Does it open windows? Let in light? Root you in values worth carrying forward? If so, it has already done its work.

And so I walk through my own evolving house — part Malay, part Western, part something new. A house of humility and hope, reflection and resilience. Some rooms are spare, others open wide to the horizon. It is still under construction, but it is a home I am learning to inhabit with grace.

The architecture of self is never complete.

What we release becomes space.
What we reclaim becomes structure.
And what we love becomes light.

Chapter 7

Hosting Souls

"And the day came when the risk to remain tight in a bud was more painful than the risk it took to blossom."
— Anaïs Nin

The New Form

In Malay culture, marriage is more than the joining of two people. It is the weaving of families, reputations, and obligations — a covenant spoken under the canopy of faith, witnessed by elders, and reinforced by generations of expectation. To marry is to honour your lineage, to carry forward the dignity of your people, to protect the honour of your parents.

And so, to divorce is not simply to part ways. It is to fracture a wider web of belonging. A daughter who leaves may be whispered about in the kampung*, her choice read as weakness or rebellion. A son may be tolerated, but the woman often bears the heavier stain. In our world, endurance is prized. Love is duty. Sacrifice is virtue.

---

* *Kampung* — A traditional Malay village community, often rural, where life is closely bound by kinship, religion, and custom.

I once thought marriage was endurance, that staying intact was the same as being whole. But sometimes what remains intact is only the structure, while the spirit has already left. Divorce carries an ache that is not only emotional but physical — the empty side of the bed, the wardrobe with gaps, the nervous system unsettled as it learns a new rhythm.

I knew this ache before I lived it. My parents divorced when I was six. I remember the silences heavier than walls, the sharpness of words, the instability of moving houses. My mother carried the doubled weight: in our community she was no longer simply a woman, but a *janda*[*] — a word that clung to her like a shadow, shrinking her worth to her marital status. My father remarried, moved on. The stain was hers alone.

So when my own marriage faltered, the grief carried more than separation. It carried inheritance. I had seen what divorce did to my mother — how she was defined not by her strength but by her rupture. Even in another country, another culture, I carried that fear.

Yet geography changes the story.

In Malaysia, divorce meant stigma. Religion framed it as failure; community made it shame. Children often lost a parent's presence along with the marriage. In the Netherlands, where I later built a life, I saw another script. Parents who had separated still stood side by side at school gates, shared birthdays, divided weeks between houses with civility. Pain was present, but not shame. Children learned family could stretch without breaking.

Elsewhere, the contrasts were starker still. In the Philippines, Catholic law makes divorce nearly impossible, binding families in permanence whether or not love remains. In Bedouin communities, divorce is permitted, but women often stayed, fearing the shame of returning to their father's tent. In Scandinavia, by

* *Janda* — In Malay culture, a term for a divorced or widowed woman. Neutral in origin, it often carries stigma in practice, unlike its male counterpart.

contrast, separation carries little stigma. Strong social safety nets soften the impact; love is seen as choice, not fate.

Anthropology reminds us even marriage itself is not one thing. Among the Na people of China, lovers come and go, with children raised by maternal uncles. Permanence was never the expectation; separation carries no shame.

And psychology teaches us this: what wounds children most is not divorce, but conflict. Research* shows that those raised in high-conflict intact families often fare worse than those whose parents separate with kindness. What matters most is presence — the assurance that love for them does not dissolve when marriage does.

Divorce, I have learned, is both grief and grace. Grief, because a story has ended. Grace, because endings can be honest too. What ended for me was not only a marriage, but also a story I had inherited: that sacrifice without reciprocity was strength, that silence was virtue, that endurance was love. Letting that story die was its own act of love — for myself, and for my daughter.

Camilla may not grow up with parents under one roof. But she will grow up knowing that love did not abandon her when marriage did. That lesson, I hope, is more enduring than the performance of togetherness.

Across cultures, the scripts differ.

Yet beneath them, the ache is universal.

To separate is to grieve. To grieve is to grow.

And to grow is to keep searching for a love honest enough to live — even if it must change form.

---

* Studies by Paul Amato and others show that children's wellbeing depends less on divorce itself than on the climate surrounding it. High-conflict intact families often cause more harm than amicable separations. Stable, supportive parenting matters most.

Nina Aziz Justin

Love Kitchen

Of all the rooms in the houses I have lived in, the kitchen has always been my favourite. It is where hunger turns into nourishment, where survival becomes ceremony, where ingredients transform into memory.

Food, for me, has never been only about eating. It is a story, a map of belonging. The flavours of my childhood still shape me: *sambal* that stings with chilli and lime; *telur kicap*, soy-sauce eggs simmered into humble comfort; *nasi goreng*, fried rice that carried the cure for the ache of migration.

Across journeys — whether migration, holiday, business trip, or a return to a city I've walked a hundred times — I have carried a ritual. I always seek out a local bookstore for a cookbook, and wander the markets for food. This is the truest way I know to understand a place: through its spices, its small cooking tricks, its heritage simmered into broth or kneaded into bread. A steaming bowl of *pho* on a Hanoi street corner, *falafel* wrapped in paper in Abu Dhabi, a baker's shared baguette secret in a French village — these encounters are not only about taste, but about listening to the soil and the people.

Over the years, I have collected recipes from friends and strangers, dishes that now live in my hands as much as in memory. My kitchen has become a crossing of worlds: *sambal* beside *soufflé*, *laksa* beside *lasagne*, each dish carrying its own geography of love.

After years of working and scaling businesses in more than forty countries, I feel I carry this archive in my very body — knowledge beyond language, a belonging written into my senses. So when I cook, I am not only feeding myself. I am recreating places, friendships, seasons of life — keeping alive every table that once welcomed me.

Food has taught me who I am, and also what others once told me was too much: too Malaysian, too spicy, too other. What I now know is that food carries my becoming as surely as memory does.

It is no surprise, then, that love with David found its meeting place around the dinner table. His French heritage brought wine, bread, and butter, the language of sauces and long meals. My Malay heart brought noodles and *sambal*, the rhythm of eating with hands and chopsticks, dishes to be shared rather than divided. Where words sometimes faltered, food spoke for us. We did not need to choose which table mattered most — we created a table of our own.

Perhaps this has always been the power of food: it lowers our guard. To eat together is to say, *you are safe here.* A shared meal has a way of weaving trust, softening edges, and making strangers into companions. Maybe this is why romance so often begins at the table.

To offer food is to offer care. To receive it is to receive love.

And then there is the mother's table. No matter how far you travel or how much you reinvent yourself, the pull of your mother's cooking is magnetic. Her food is not only flavour — it is safety, the architecture of first belonging. Even now, I long for my mother's *char kway teow*, because it carries that first lesson of love: unconditional, wordless, nourishing.

Love, then, is a kind of kitchen. A place of invention and memory, of offering and receiving. With David, I learned that our differences were not obstacles but ingredients. He did not ask me to put away my *sambal* or *telur kicap*. I did not ask him to give up his cheeses or his bread. What bound us was not sameness, but the willingness to let what was distinct simmer into something shared.

I remember the first time he tasted my cooking. I had toned down the spice in a *rendang*, worried it might overwhelm him. He took a bite, smiled, and said, "It isn't spicy enough." In that moment, I laughed with relief. He wasn't asking me to dilute myself. He was inviting me to bring my full flavour to the table.

Love, I realised, is not the absence of heat — it is the willingness to taste it together.

Tending Fire

Motherhood did not arrive in a vacuum. I carried into it the weight of my culture's expectations — the Malay scripts where a woman's worth was measured, in part, by her children. To be called *ibu** was to be crowned with reverence, to embody sacrifice and service. Lullabies, the forty days of *pantang*† after birth, the shared wisdom of women in kitchens and *suraus*‡ all taught me that motherhood was destiny fulfilled.

But Europe told me another story. In the Netherlands, mothers cycled to work with babies strapped to handlebars, children slept in prams outside cafés, and families spoke openly about boundaries and balance. In France, motherhood unfolded with refinement: food, manners, rituals of education.

I lived between these worlds — one where motherhood was sacred duty, and another where it was a choice among many. To mother in this in-between space was both gift and tension. I wanted to honour the reverence of my heritage without losing myself in its sacrifice. I wanted to embrace the freedoms of Europe without dismissing the tenderness of tradition.

And yet, I have come to believe that motherhood is only one way of hosting souls. For some it is children. For others it is communities, friendships, students, or creative work. Each of us carries something larger than ourselves, something that asks us to stretch, to hold a flame, to keep a hearth burning wide enough for what has chosen us.

---

* *Ibu* — Malay for "mother," a title of reverence. Used not only for women who bear children but also for elders and caregivers, and even for the land itself: *Ibu Pertiwi* means "Mother Earth" or "Motherland."

† *Pantang* — the forty-day Malay postpartum practice of rest and recovery. It includes herbal baths, body massage, binding, and special diets, meant to restore strength and protect mother and child. It reflects both tenderness and expectation: women recover not only for themselves but for the families who depend on them.

‡ *Surau* — A small Muslim prayer house in Malaysia and Indonesia. Unlike a larger mosque, a surau is intimate, serving not only for prayer but as a gathering place for storytelling, teaching, and the passing on of women's and elders' wisdom.

For me, Camilla and Isabel were never tenants of a foundation but sparks that illuminated hidden corners of myself. They are not mine to own, but fireflies passing through on their way into the night sky. Kahlil Gibran wrote that children "come through you but not from you." I have come to know that truth in my bones.

Camilla arrived like a sudden flame, showing me that love could blaze brighter than my fear of repeating the past. Isabel followed, her rare condition reshaping me with a slower glow, a light that burned from the inside out. My daughters are not my possessions but my teachers. They do not live in my house so much as they have lit its rooms with their fire.

Motherhood, I realise, is not about laying down a foundation for them to stand on. It is about tending their fire — so that when the time comes, they can carry light into places I will never reach.

The Ancestral House.

"Try to accept the changing seasons of your soul, even as you have always accepted the passing of the days. The house of your being was never meant to stay the same." – Rumi

To become a mother is never only to welcome a child. It is also to remember that you were once a child yourself.

With every lullaby I sang to Camilla, I heard the echo of my mother's voice. With every meal I prepared for Isabel, I recalled the dishes placed before me. Motherhood does not open just one room — it opens the ancestral house. Suddenly you are walking its corridors, hearing voices that shaped you long before you knew you would one day carry children of your own.

In the Malay world, the ancestral house is both literal and symbolic. It is the wooden home raised on stilts, with spaces divided for ceremony, for prayer, for sleep, for cooking. It is also the house of lineage, where each generation carries the weight of the last.

To step into motherhood is to remember: you do not begin from emptiness. You begin from inheritance.

I remember my maternal grandmother, Wan Peah, not for long conversations — she often forgot my name after raising more than ten children, some lost to tropical diseases and miscarriage. Sometimes she could not recall which daughter was my mother. And yet I remember her clearly, always in her kitchen, always rolling the heavy *batu giling** — the stone grinder used for spices — her arms steady with the rhythm of someone who had done it for a lifetime. The kitchen was her sanctuary, filled with turmeric and lemongrass, a place where she spoke less with words than with food. We, her grandchildren, were told to be quiet while she worked, and so we watched in silence as her strength became our inheritance.

But inheritance is never neutral. Some rooms are filled with tenderness, others with agony. Some doors open to comfort, others creak with judgment.

In my ancestral house, I inherited both: the warmth of meals, the cadence of lullabies, the resilience of women who endured. But also the weight of reticence, and its opposite — the feistiness expected of the women in our family, their fierce words narrowing rather than widening. My mother's strength has always been my barometer, even when her disapproval pressed against me like a closed door.

Motherhood asks us to choose which rooms to leave open for our children, and which to quietly close. I wanted Camilla and Isabel to inherit the rhythm of Malay lullabies, the sacredness of prayer, the resilience of the women before them — but not the shadows that shrink a girl's joy because of her darker skin, nor the

* The *batu giling* is a traditional Malay stone grinder, consisting of a large flat slab and a heavy rolling pin–like stone. For generations, it was used to grind fresh spices, curry pastes, and chilli blends by hand. Its rhythmic labour infused food with both flavour and memory, becoming a quiet emblem of endurance and care.

quiet patterns of silence that teach compliance at the cost of her voice.

Ancestral houses are not fixed.

They can be rearranged, reimagined.

To mother is not simply to pass down everything we were given, but to discern what deserves to live on and what must be released.

My daughters do not need every room preserved. They need spaces wide enough to become who they are meant to be, not who I or the women before me wished them to become.

They are children of the future, not custodians of my past.

Their house will have many extensions, stretching into new lands, with windows I could never design, opening toward horizons I may never reach. And perhaps that is the true work of lineage: not to replicate what was, but to create new rooms of belonging wherever life plants us.

Each generation does not return to the same room, but circles back differently — altered, expanded, carrying both memory and possibility.

Mama

"Kasih ibu membawa ke syurga." —
A mother's love carries you to heaven.
~ Malay Proverb

Mothers do not only pass down recipes and lullabies. They also pass down their silences, their judgments, their hopes wrapped in worry. My own mother carried a deep well of strength, but hers was shaped by endurance. In her eyes, a woman's worth was measured not by freedom but by sacrifice — by keeping the family intact, no matter the cost.

When my marriage with Camilla's father dissolved, her disappointment was palpable. She did not shout or curse. Her disapproval was true to her character. Quieter, sharper — like a door that would not open. I knew she worried for me, feared for Camilla, concerned the shame that divorce still carried in our Malay world. For her, endurance was not just virtue. It was survival.

Her hopes for me were shaped by her own wounds. After her divorce from my father, she had been frowned upon, her dignity questioned in ways no woman should endure. That stigma followed her for years, and perhaps it explains why she often measured me against the children of others — not when I excelled, but when I was different.

When I left for England, she expected me to return home triumphant, to be an accolade for her sacrifice — proof to the world that she was not inferior, but extraordinary, having raised successful children against the odds.

My choice not to return was, for her, at first a source of pain, perhaps even humiliation. In our culture*, daughters are expected to care for their mothers in their later years. To choose otherwise is rare, and for me it has always carried a trace of guilt, an ache that has never quite left me, to this day.

And yet, I knew I had to choose myself. I could not live as my mother's do-over, carrying the dreams she could not fulfil. I had to renovate the ancestral blueprint, even when it meant tearing down patterns that had defined women in my family for generations.

In time, she accepted my decision, though not without an intermittent grudge that has kept our relationship tender but never entirely easy. As she has grown older and more devout in her Islamic faith, she sometimes reminds me of how far I have drifted from what she hoped.

I understand her longing. She wanted a mirror to restore her

* In many Asian cultures, caring for aging parents is considered a sacred duty rather than a choice. Rooted in Confucian, Hindu, and Islamic traditions, filial piety is seen as repayment for the sacrifices parents made in raising their children.

dignity in the eyes of others. What she received instead was a daughter who could not be her reflection, only herself.

And so, between us lies both love and distance.

She gave me strength, and she gave me weight.

I honour her resilience even as I release the ambivalence she carried. To mother my own daughters is to walk this delicate line — to carry forward the tenderness that nourishes, but not the shame that diminishes.

In the end, my mother and I are bound not by perfect agreement but by the unspoken truth that love insists on its own form.

Sometimes it is laughter around the table.

Sometimes a prayer whispered in different languages.

Sometimes it is simply this: no matter how far I roam, a part of me will always be my Mama's daughter — still learning to love her as she is, and hoping she might love me as I am.

Noor

> *"He is Al-Rahman, the Compassionate; Al-Hafiz, the Protector; Al-Nur, the Light."*
>
> — Asma'ul Husna

Faith has always been part of the air I breathe. From the azan* that floated across my childhood evenings to the *zikr*† we attended on Thursday nights at boarding school in Raub — belief was not a lesson but a rhythm.

To grow up Malay and Muslim was to grow up inside a prayer.

---

* The *azan* (or *adhan*) is the Muslim call to prayer, recited five times daily. Its melodic phrases — beginning with "Allahu Akbar," meaning "God is the Greatest" — weave devotion into the rhythm of community life.

† ∗ *Zikr* (or *dhikr*) means "remembrance" in Arabic and refers to the devotional repetition of God's names or phrases of praise, performed aloud or silently, alone or in community.

Yet life carried me into lands where faith spoke in other tongues. In Europe, I heard church bells toll the hours. I watched French mothers teach their children to fold hands before bread and wine. In the Netherlands, spirituality was quieter, more private — yet its silence was its own kind of presence.

Motherhood brought these contrasts into sharper focus. Rocking Camilla to sleep, I hummed lullabies stitched with prayer. With Isabel, I whispered *'Bismillah'* * before every medical procedure — not from obligation, but because prayer was the language my body reached for when I longed to protect them.

One evening, Camilla — still so small her fingers barely wrapped around mine — asked if I could teach her how to pray. I told her that prayer was gratitude for what is good, and a plea for protection from what harms. She nodded, then looked up at me with the candour only children carry:

"Where is God? Who is God?"

I did not want to give her a lecture or words too heavy for a child. So I pointed her back to the magic she already knew:

"God is in the kindness that makes you feel safe.

In the hug that warms you.

In the stars that keep shining even when you can't count them all.

In the way the wind carries the sound.

In the love that never leaves."

She smiled with satisfaction — and in that smile I saw what I had almost forgotten: that children understand mystery more easily than certainty. For them, God is not an idea to be defended but a wonder to be felt.

Since then, I have come to believe that our lives themselves can be prayer. The way we speak, the choices we make, the tenderness we show — all of it can be an offering. To live with

* *Bismillahirrahmanirrahim* — "In the name of God, the Most Compassionate, the Most Merciful." This phrase opens nearly every chapter of the Qur'an and is recited to begin daily acts with God's mercy and love.

compassion, forgiveness, and mercy is to echo God's beautiful names, the *Asma'ul Husna**, in daily life.

Every act of care is remembrance.

Every act of love is worship.

And yet, so much of the world still moves on an "us versus them" axis. I have seen this in the East and the West alike. Such separation forgets that God is not bound to one people or one place.

God is *Al-Rahman,* the Compassionate; *Al-Rahim,* the Merciful — wide enough to hold us all. Every time I say *Bismillahirrahmanirrahim,* I remember: God's nature is love, limitless and encompassing.

There are those who, because of the way I hold my faith, have called me less than Muslim. Yet what they saw as distance became, for me, a deepening. Islam did not diminish when I embraced it through kindness and presence; it widened, glowed, became more radiant. To be Muslim, I have come to believe, is to see God not only in ritual but in the quiet thread of goodness woven through nature, His creation and daily life.

This is what I want my daughters to know: God is never absent. God is the nearness of love, the presence that steadies them when the world feels uncertain.

Prayer, I have learned, is not only about faith. It is also about belonging. A mother whispering *bismillah* before feeding her child, a father blessing bread with wine, a grandmother lighting a candle — each is saying,

You are held by something larger than me.

Prayer becomes the invisible shelter we build around the ones we love.

* *Asma'ul Husna* — "the Most Beautiful Names" — are the 99 attributes of God described in the Qur'an, each reflecting a Divine quality such as compassion, protection, or light.

And so, across cultures, I began to see prayer not as a dividing line, but as an all encompassing light — *Noor**.

Both my daughters carry Noor as their middle name, a reminder that they inherit not one tradition but many languages of love: Malay, Dutch, English, Arabic, French, and the unspoken ones too.

What I want them to know is this: no matter where they are, or which words they choose, prayer is less about the form than the remembering. It is the eternal refrain, carried across faiths and generations:

You are never alone.

The light is always here.

The Seamless Self

For years I tried to divide myself into tidy boxes. Mother here. Professional there. Malay-Muslim in this room. Migrant in that one. As if life could be stacked neatly, one identity never spilling into another.

But compartments are an illusion. Motherhood leaks into work. Work shadows faith. Culture seeps into love. Even silence speaks across borders. Neuroscience tells us the brain does not store life in sealed chambers. It weaves experience together, memory not in drawers but in tapestries.

And yet society loves compartments. The West speaks of "work–life balance," as if life could be balanced like an accountant's ledger. In Asia, roles are scripted so tightly that to step outside one feels like betrayal. Everywhere the message is the same: if only we managed our boxes better, we would finally be whole.

---

* *Noor* (also spelled *Nur*) is the Arabic word for "light," often understood in Islamic faith as the light of God — illumination, guidance, and divine presence. It appears in the Qur'an, such as in the famous *Ayat an-Nur* (24:35), "Allah is the Light of the heavens and the earth." As a name, it carries connotations of radiance, hope, and spiritual clarity, symbolising both inner and outer light.

I have always struggled with this. My ambition for work was as fierce as my devotion to motherhood. Sometimes I wondered if this hunger was a flaw — or simply the survival instinct of a foreigner, working harder to justify why I lived oceans away from the ease of Malaysia. Perhaps it was the emptiness of a marriage already cracking. Perhaps it was ego. Perhaps it was the gift of Lelde, our extraordinary nanny, who became a sister to both Camilla and me. Likely it was all of these at once.

When Camilla was little, my life was measured in airports and boarding gates. I scaled businesses across continents, first for other start-ups and then my own. Some months I woke up in four time zones, my suitcase always half-packed. And yet, no matter how far I traveled, I flew home for the things that mattered: her birthdays, her school report cards, her ballet recitals, the evening Sinterklaas* knocked at our door. For a season, it worked.

But seasons change. My marriage to Camilla's father collapsed, and with David came a different rhythm. When Isabel was born — and with her, the rare TRIP12 condition† — my pace shifted. Life slowed, deepened. The old rules of balance no longer applied.

Motherhood revealed that the boxes had never been real. Camilla and Isabel did not wait until I finished work to need me. My prayers did not pause because I was traveling. Isabel's laughter healed in ways no boardroom could. Camilla's questions

---

* *Sinterklaas*, or Saint Nicholas, is a beloved Dutch figure whose feast is celebrated on 5 December (*pakjesavond*, or "present evening"). He arrives from Spain by steamboat in November, parades on a white horse, and brings gifts. For Dutch children, *Sinterklaas* is often more important than Christmas itself, anchoring family rituals and cultural memory.

† *TRIP12 syndrome* is an ultra-rare genetic neurodevelopmental condition caused by changes in the TRIP12 gene, which plays a role in brain development. Fewer than a few hundred cases are known worldwide. Children often experience developmental delays, intellectual disability, and low muscle tone, with presentations varying widely. Families face long journeys to diagnosis, and medical knowledge is still emerging.

about why her mixed heritage made her stand out taught me more about belonging than any academic paper.

Looking back, I see that none of it was wasted. Every choice — even the imperfect ones — was simply me doing the best I could with what I knew. Each season carried its own education. Some taught me ambition. Some taught me endurance. Some taught me surrender.

Integration, I have learned, is not weakness. It is wisdom. To live as one seamless self is to reject the myth of division. To say: I am not fragments. I am whole. Every pivot is its own education. Every season its own teacher.

Joy and Struggle

Motherhood is often described in extremes. In some narratives it is pure calling, in others pure burden. In my truth, it is both: sometimes a strategy that sharpens us, sometimes an interference that interrupts us, always a presence that changes with the seasons.

When Camilla was little, motherhood became the lens through which I negotiated ambition. Every choice was weighed against her needs, every opportunity measured not only in profit but in presence. She gave my drive clarity, even as she also gave it limits. My career was not built in spite of motherhood but alongside it, as if the two were in constant conversation, shaping each other's contours.

And yet, there were days it felt like interference. When I boarded another plane, when I dialled into meetings while half of me remained at home, when guilt pressed heavy on my chest. Society told me I could "have it all," but having it all often meant being torn apart in the process.

Different cultures framed this tension in their own ways.

In much of Asia, motherhood is still honoured as sacred duty, a crown that dignifies a woman, measured by endurance and sacrifice. Yet in the same Malaysia I grew up in, many mothers never considered giving up work — providing itself was love, a way to ensure children never felt lack*.

In the West, by contrast, motherhood is often framed as choice, even as a stage for self-actualisation: protect your freedom, keep your identity, do not disappear into duty. Neither story guarantees happiness. Both carry beauty, both carry burden.

What matters most, psychology reminds us, is not the script we inherit but how we interpret it†. Mothers who accept the path they have taken, who can see meaning in both sacrifice and freedom, report greater resilience than those who feel trapped by the role. Joy and struggle walk hand in hand, but perception determines how heavy the walk feels.

Isabel, with her rare diagnosis, deepened this lesson. She taught me that strategy is not always expansion. Sometimes it is contraction — a deliberate narrowing, an interference that insists you slow down, stay present, listen differently. What once felt like disruption became its own kind of wisdom, redirecting me toward what mattered most.

Motherhood, I have learned, is neither only strategy nor only interference. It is both, and more. It interrupts the life you thought you were building and teaches you to build another, one truer to the soul. The best path is not to measure your life against the choices of others, East or West, but to walk your own with open hands. For happiness is not found in the script itself, but in the way we choose to live it.

---

* In many Asian cultures, providing materially for children is considered one of the highest forms of parental duty. Work is seen not as a distraction from motherhood but as part of it, ensuring dignity, education, and opportunity. Western parenting ideals often emphasise time spent with children as the ultimate marker of love. Both models reflect different values around duty, love, and survival.

† Research shows that parental wellbeing is shaped less by circumstance than by perception. Studies on "cognitive appraisal" (Lazarus & Folkman, 1984) demonstrate that how parents interpret their role — as burden or opportunity — strongly influences resilience. Sonja Lyubomirsky, in *The How of Happiness* (2007), notes that up to 40 percent of happiness depends not on external conditions but on intentional mindset and daily practice.

Magnified Fractures

Motherhood does not happen in isolation. It lays its weight on every bond around it, especially the intimate ones.

Love that once flowed freely is suddenly asked to share space with sleepless nights, unspoken resentments, shifting roles. What was once a duet becomes a crowded chorus, where exhaustion often drowns out harmony.

I have known this fracture.

With Camilla's father, silence grew louder with each year, until even birthdays and shared responsibilities could not mask the emptiness. We were both trying — but often in parallel, rarely in unison. Looking back, I see now that motherhood did not cause the collapse. It simply revealed the fault lines already there. Pain wears many faces. The ache beneath has always been the same — the longing to be met.

Later, with David, the terrain was different. Isabel's arrival, and her diagnosis, placed us on uncharted ground. There were moments of closeness so steadying that I felt cradled in his presence. And there were seasons when grief and fatigue carved distance between us. Motherhood has a way of magnifying everything — tenderness and tension alike.

Across cultures, these fractures are held differently. Every generation builds its own vocabulary for this truth.

In Asia today, many women can choose for themselves, yet the choice is rarely made in isolation. It is shaped by whether she can support herself, whether her community will stand with her, whether her family constellation allows independence. In the West, choice can appear easier, but it too is nuanced. In England, I saw how the invisible scaffolding of class still decides who can truly stand on her own*. In the Netherlands, I discovered another

* In Britain, class still lingers like an unspoken script. It shapes accents and schools, careers and futures.

story: here, systems of support catch not only women but children too, so that separation need not mean collapse*.

I have never believed one way is better than another. Every story is written within its own limits and its own possibilities. But I know I have been blessed. My children have grown in lands where their safety was protected, where even in the wake of fracture they could find joy. This is a gift not every mother can count on, and it humbles me.

Fractures are painful, but they are also teachers. They remind us that love is not static. It requires repair, renewal, sometimes release. The body heals by knitting itself anew; so too must relationships find ways to grow stronger at the broken places, or to accept that some walls cannot be rebuilt.

And love itself — wherever it is found — remains human. It is not defined by race or geography, nor by the coordinates where two people meet. It is the same pulse that beats across cultures, the same longing to be seen and held.

However different the stories we inherit, the truth of love belongs to all of us.

Love has no homeland but the human heart.

Resentments and Realignments

Not all fractures arrive with noise.

Some slip in quietly, like shadows in a room.

They gather in the pauses between conversations, in the small disappointments never spoken, in the exhaustion that leaves no space for tenderness. These are the quiet resentments — not the kind that shatter walls, but the kind that slowly shift their foundations.

* Studies by UNICEF and the OECD often place Dutch children among the happiest in the world — not because their parents are always together, but because the culture around them safeguards their wellbeing, giving joy room to breathe even when families fracture.

Motherhood, with its relentless demands, often exposes these shadows. The imbalance of care. The invisible labour. The way one partner carries more of the daily weight while the other shoulders more of the world outside. None of it is done with malice, yet the effect is the same: a subtle erosion of intimacy, a feeling of being unseen.

Resentment is not confined to marriages. In my family, it tends to be hidden from the naked eye. Everyone wants to appear loving and kind, as polished as the perfect Instagram grid — or, in my mother's generation, the carefully composed family portrait, framed to suggest harmony even when silence filled the space between us. But beneath these surfaces, there is more drama than anyone admits. My mother's siblings, who inherited a large piece of land from my grandparents, have long been caught in a web of unspoken rivalries. My cousins and I often joke that their quarrels are like an ancient knot — tangled for so long that no one remembers how the threads were first pulled tight. None of us wants to inherit that land, except for the fact that in Asian families rejecting a gift is seen as an insult. And so we smile, nod, and carry burdens we would rather put down, because keeping harmony matters more than honesty.

Anthropologists have long written about this contrast between cultures. In Asia, and in Mediterranean countries like France, harmony and image are prized. Conflict is often addressed indirectly — through nuance, politeness, or silence. The goal is to preserve relationships, even at the cost of truth.

In more individualistic cultures, such as the Netherlands, confrontation is less feared. People sit down, name the problem, and try to resolve it openly. The goal is clarity, even if it leaves scars. Neither approach is perfect. One avoids rupture but accumulates tension; the other clears the air but risks the wound of bluntness.

In my own life, I have seen both. In Malaysia, where silence protects image, resentments simmer like hidden embers. In Holland, where directness is prized, differences are laid bare and often resolved, though never without ache. What I have learned is that resentment, wherever it appears, is rarely about the surface issue. It is about the longing to be seen, to be heard, to matter.

And yet even resentment carries its own invitation. It asks us to notice what has been ignored. It urges us to speak what has been left unsaid. Sometimes only through discomfort are we pushed toward realignment, toward a truer form of love. Sacred realignments rarely arrive with fanfare. They arrive in the decision to stay present, to forgive, to notice one another again. They live in the willingness to repair, even imperfectly. Perhaps this is the quiet miracle of love: that beneath resentment lies the possibility of renewal, if we dare to name the ache and choose again.

In many Asian families, this tension is softened beneath the cultural practice of "*saving face." It means preserving dignity and social harmony, even when it costs honesty. To reject a gift, to confront too directly, or to expose a conflict can bring shame not only to the individual but to the wider family. Politeness and image become protective layers, keeping relationships intact on the surface, even while tensions quietly smolder underneath.

And perhaps this is what realignment ultimately teaches: that even in the quiet fractures of family, friendship, or marriage, the work of becoming continues. To face the shadow, to repair or release, is to widen the frame of love itself.

Each time we choose truth over pretense, tenderness over pride, the home within gains another room — not perfect, not polished, but real enough to embrace us.

---

* In many Asian cultures, "saving face" refers to preserving dignity, honour, and social harmony in the eyes of others. It often means avoiding open conflict, refusing to embarrass someone publicly, or accepting gifts even when they bring burden. To reject a gift or to confront a family member too directly may be seen as disrespectful, creating shame not only for the individual but for the wider family. Politeness and image become protective layers, keeping relationships intact on the surface, even when tension runs quietly underneath.

Renewal

We often forget that while we build with our hands, there is always 'the hands' we cannot see, shaping what endures and what falls away. From the time we are young, we are told that we are powerful — the captains of our ships, the architects of our destiny. We imagine ourselves drawing blueprints, laying bricks, making plans.

But there is a flaw in this thinking. Effort is essential, yes, but so is surrender. Life does not yield to our designs alone. To live fully is to flex, to soften the ego, to accept that the most important things are not in our hands.

In the Islamic tradition, the *Hand of Fatima** is a reminder of blessing and protection — a symbol that what shields us is not our will alone but God's mercy. In many cultures we speak of *kismet,*† the unfolding of destiny, the truth that some paths are written beyond our control.

And so, sometimes life arrives like a storm, tearing down what we thought was permanent, leaving us in the rubble of our own expectations. That is when rebuilding begins — not only by our effort, but by the hidden insistence of life itself.

Divorce stripped me of the story I thought I was living. Motherhood rewrote my rhythm, demanding rooms I had never imagined. And Isabel, my younger daughter, called me into an even deeper reinvention of self. Her rare neurological condition reshaped not only my priorities but my environment.

I found myself rethinking where and how we lived, especially when I saw how some people changed toward us. Children who once played freely grew distant, their parents drawing back as if Isabel's difference might be contagious. She was labelled strange,

---

* *The Hand of Fatima,* also known as the Hamsa, is a palm-shaped amulet across the Middle East and North Africa, symbolising protection, patience, and blessing — a reminder that safety rests not only in human effort but in divine care.

† *Kismet,* from the Arabic *qisma* meaning portion or lot, speaks of destiny — a balance between striving and surrender, a comfort and a call to humility

sometimes excluded — not because of who she was, but because she did not fit neatly into the world's idea of normal.

Cultural differences made these experiences even more complex. In Malaysia, children like Isabel are often called *anak syurga* *— children of heaven. There is reverence in that name, a recognition that they carry innocence and light. Families raising them are met with empathy, community support, and spiritual affirmation, even when formal services remain limited.

In the Netherlands, the story is different. Here, it is not society or extended family that carries most of the weight, but the state. Government systems provide therapies, integration programs, and education pathways that make sure families like mine do not live entirely on the fringe. Both approaches have their beauty and their gaps. In Malaysia, compassion comes from community, but resources are scarce. In Europe, resources are abundant, but empathy in daily life is not always guaranteed.

Between these two worlds I found myself continually being remade. Renewal was not a single event but an unending practice, and it was often painful. Shedding old identities felt like shedding skin. I cried at the smallest things: a playground exclusion, a friend's thoughtless remark, the sight of a stranger having a simple conversation with their child. I no longer knew how to introduce myself, because the roles I once wore had dissolved. Was I still an entrepreneur, a business strategist, a wife, a traveller — or only a mother learning to navigate a world I had never entered before?

This new world took me to unexpected places. I stood at benefit concerts organised by my friend Monica, a musician who used her gift to support children bound to wheelchairs for life. Surrounded by those families, I felt both heartbreak and belonging. I began to walk long distances as a way to breathe through the weight of change. I lived with low-grade depression for years,

* In Malay, *anak syurga* — "children of heaven" — is a term of reverence for children with disabilities, recognising innocence and purity. Community empathy often flows freely, even when formal services remain scarce.

carrying its heaviness like an invisible cloak. To steady myself, I practised yoga daily, finding small anchors in breath and movement. I travelled to a silent ashram in India, hoping that stillness might reveal the strength to face a life that no longer followed my design.

Science* reminds us that change, even chosen change, unsettles the brain. It disrupts our neural pathways and forces us into uncertainty. Yet it is through this very disruption that neuro-plasticity takes root, allowing the mind to grow new connections — just as broken bones grow calluses to strengthen the fracture.

I recognised in this what the Sufis and Taoists had always known: that what feels like breaking is, in truth, an opening. The wound is where the light enters. To yield is not to lose but to endure. Renewal demands that we bend, break, and bend again.

It took not weeks but years to find my footing, and I am still being remade. Renewal is not only stark in my story, but seasonal in everyone's. Each of us is asked to reinvent ourselves again and again, whether through motherhood, illness, love, loss, or simply the passing of time. Renewal is the curriculum of life itself.

Life has rebuilt me repeatedly. It has taken away marriages, plans, and identities, and given me in return daughters who redefined love, friendships that became family, and a home no longer bound by geography but rooted within. Perhaps this is the heart of renewal: we are not only builders, we are also the ones being built. Life chisels away what no longer fits, widening the frame for what is yet to come. And if we are tender enough to let it, every dismantling carries within it the blueprint of a greater wholeness.

Renewal is not proof of our power, but of a wisdom greater than us, forever reshaping the house of our lives. And perhaps this is the deeper invitation: to trust that even in the collapse, the foundations of the home within are being quietly laid anew.

---

* Neuroscience shows that change unsettles but also strengthens. Neuro-plasticity allows the brain to grow new pathways in the face of disruption — much like a fracture healing stronger at the broken place.

Chapter 8

Self-Cartography

Tongue-Tied by Borders

When Camilla was born, I wanted her first language to be English. It was not a random choice but an echo of my own childhood. My mother, schooled in English in the last decade of British rule in Malaya, raised my brother Dzul and me bilingually.

At home, English was not only language but ritual. We had "English Thursdays," when we were fined ten cents for every Malay word we spoke. Dzul usually kept silent that day, saving his pocket money in stubborn quiet. I embraced it with enthusiasm, eager to practice. My parents even argued in English, a deliberate code to keep our house helpers from understanding. To this day, when I feel anger or disappointment, I still revert to English with my parents. It became my first language of emotion, even though Malay holds more words for tenderness, affection, and love.

Languages are not equal in what they hold. In Malay there is *cinta* for romantic love, *kasih* for tenderness, *sayang* for affection and fondness, *mesra* for intimacy, *rindu* for longing, *asmara* for desire*. Each word is a different key on the piano of love. English collapses many of them into one: *love.*

Other languages carry their own untranslatables. The Germans gave us *schadenfreude*† — the guilty pleasure of another's misfortune. The Portuguese hold *saudade*‡ — the bittersweet ache of longing for something absent but still beloved. Each word is not only vocabulary but culture, a window into what a community has felt so often that it needed to be named.

To lose a language is to lose not only grammar but access to certain shades of human experience. To gain one is to inherit new colours for the soul. Perhaps this is why grief for a slipping language feels so deep. It is not just words leaving. It is an entire emotional landscape receding from reach.

I raised Camilla in English, believing it would give her a language she could use anywhere in the world. She proudly told people that English was her mother tongue, though sometimes with confusion. "But Mama, you're not English," she would protest, puzzled that I was Malaysian, educated in England only later in life.

Still, Dutch soon wrapped itself around her daily life: the language of the playground, of teachers and friendships. She became bilingual, English and Dutch layered like two skins. I still sang to my daughters in Malay — *Burung Kakak Tua, Rasa Sayang, Bintang Kecil*§ — lullabies from my own childhood. Camilla giggled at the playful word *busuk* #("smelly"), a pet name whispered to children. But Malay was never her anchor. My grief was not only about words lost, but about what those words carried: stories, songs, kitchens, prayers.

---

* *Cinta, kasih, sayang, mesra, rindu, asmara*: Malay has a rich emotional palette for love, each word its own shade of affection.

† *Schadenfreude*: German, "harm-joy" — pleasure in another's misfortune.

‡ *Saudade*: Portuguese, a bittersweet longing for something absent yet beloved.

§ *Burung Kakak Tua, Rasa Sayang, Bintang Kecil*: nursery songs sung across the Malay archipelago, carrying childhood comfort and cultural memory.

\# *Busuk*: literally "smelly," but in Malay, often a term of endearment for children.

Languages are never static. They are rivers, carrying the sediments of history as they move. To speak one is to step into its history. To migrate is to step into another. And to raise children between them is to watch new rivers form, braiding streams that could never have existed without the crossing.

Perhaps that is why learning a language is never only about memorising words. It is about feeling its rhythm in your mouth, letting its metaphors shape your imagination. Migrants know this well: you cannot belong in a language until you allow yourself to feel it. To love in French, to pray in Malay, to grieve in English — each one rewires the soul in its own way.

And so, when Camilla answered me in English, I came to see it not as rejection of Malay but as evolution. Just as my mother passed English to me to widen my world, I passed it to Camilla with the same hope. What we hand down is never identical. It is adapted, translated, reshaped by the soil it falls into. Camilla's English is not mine. Her Dutch is not mine. But both are hers, and through them, she is writing a story I could never have written, even if I had tried.

Beyond Words

"To learn a language is to have one more window from which to look at the world."
— Chinese proverb

Belonging is not only about passports or postcodes. It is also about the words that live in our hearts.

When Camilla spoke to me in English, always and without exception, I felt no regret. I had chosen that path for her, believing it would give her a language she could carry anywhere in the world. And yet, sometimes I wondered what it might have been like if she could also shape her mouth around Malay — not only to taste its words but to feel them in her skin.

Language is never just vocabulary; it is a way of being. I wished she could share more of that side of my heritage with me — not only through food and stories, but through the music of the tongue itself.

Yet languages, like families, are never static. They evolve with the journeys they carry. Just as Malay absorbed words from Sanskrit, Arabic, Portuguese, and Chinese, and just as English gathered fragments from French and Latin, so too do our family languages shift across borders. What we pass on is always a new version of what was given to us.

Would she ever know how *rasa sayang*[*] is more than "feeling of love," how *kasih* carries a tenderness that no single English word can hold?

But belonging cannot be forced. Languages, like roots, grow only where the soil is ready. What I had to learn was the art of letting go. To trust that even if she never spoke Malay fluently, she could still carry its spirit — in the food she ate, in the stories she heard, in the way my love wrapped her childhood.

Isabel's path with language was different. Because of her rare neurological syndrome, words came slowly, haltingly, and always with their own creativity. She mixed the languages of her environment, borrowing whichever word felt easiest in her mouth. Linguists call this *code-switching*[†] — not confusion, but creativity, the weaving together of tongues into one living fabric.

Isabel would say *l'avion* for aeroplane in French, skipping over the heavier Dutch *vliegtuig*. On rainy days she would announce *c'est nat* — *c'est* in French for "it is," blended with *nat*, Dutch for "wet." She called me *Maman* in French, even as Camilla calls me *Mummy* and I call myself *Mama*. Her voice was a mosaic of languages, stitched together by instinct and need.

---

* *Rasa sayang*: more than "feeling of love," it carries the joy of affection woven through Malay culture.

† *Code-switching*: when multilingual children blend languages in a single phrase — not confusion, but creativity.

And then, at five, her speech disappeared altogether due to her neurological condition. We watched the words fade from her mouth until there were none left. With the loss of her speech, it felt as though we were being asked to learn a new language from the beginning — one without syllables, one carried in looks, gestures, and presence.

At first, there was stabbing grief in that silence. But slowly, I began to see that she had not fallen silent at all. She was teaching me another way of communicating, one that did not depend on vocabulary.

This, too, is what mothering across borders has taught me: that language is fluid, not fixed. Some words are lost, others invented. Some conversations happen in French, Dutch, or English. Others happen in silence, in the language of eyes, touch, and patience. Each shift is a reminder that belonging is not about holding on to a single tongue but about finding ways to connect, again and again.

Science* tells us that every language we carry shapes not only how we think but how we feel. To be bilingual or multilingual is to hold multiple ways of perceiving the world. To lose a language is not only to lose words, but a way of seeing. And yet, to gain a new one is to expand the mind, to stretch the heart toward another horizon.

Isabel reminds me of this every day: that belonging does not depend on words, and that sometimes the deepest truths require no words at all. Letting go of a language does not mean erasure. It means allowing belonging to find its own form, even in silence.

Perhaps the real mother tongue is not the first language we speak, but the way we learn to understand and be understood.

* Research shows each language we carry shapes not just thought, but feeling; bilingual minds hold multiple ways of seeing.

Mosaics

My daughters are mosaics*, each tile cut from a different world. At home, they grow within a tapestry of cultures — Malay, French, English — a house where values mix as naturally as spices in a pot. Yet outside our doors, their childhood has been quintessentially Dutch. They learned to ride bikes before they could tie their shoes. They sat in school circles where every child had a turn to speak, their voices counted as much as an adult's. Here, children are treated as equals in the making, taught to question even their teachers, to speak up if something feels unfair, to trust that the system will protect them.

This openness stands in contrast to how I was raised in Malaysia, where children's voices were expected to be soft. We learned *budi bahasa*† and *adab*‡ — refined speech and respectful conduct — as the foundation of character. To talk back to an elder was *kurang ajar*§, a mark not only on the child but on the parents. Silence was not failure; it was virtue.

Dutch life has left its imprint on them. Camilla negotiates boundaries with the bluntness of her peers, certain that her voice belongs in every room. Once, she came home and told David with wide-eyed certainty, "Papa, France has just now allowed homosexual marriages. Here, they've been allowing that since forever!"# To her, equality was not a debate, but the natural order of things. Isabel, meanwhile, has been nurtured in a special needs school where play is central and pressure is gentle, where expectations

---

* *Mosaic* — an artwork of many pieces, each distinct yet belonging to a luminous whole; here, a metaphor for children shaped by many cultures.

† *Budi bahasa* — refined speech and politeness; in Malay culture, a mirror of character.

‡ *Adab* — manners and respect rooted in Islamic teaching; the fabric of family honour.

§ *Kurang ajar* — literally "poorly taught," used when children speak out of turn; shorthand for disrespect.

In 2001, the Netherlands became the first country to legalise same-sex marriage; for Dutch children, equality is simply the norm.

are adjusted with kindness instead of force. She has been allowed to grow at her own pace, and to be accepted as she is.

And then there is the Dutch habit of offering opinions freely. Strangers in the park or at the supermarket will sometimes advise me how to care for Isabel, with the sincerity of people who truly believe they are helping, even when no advice was asked for. It can be disarming, sometimes amusing, but it springs from the same soil that teaches children to speak up: a conviction that voices should be used, that silence is rarely necessary.

Living in the Netherlands has also shown me how childhood differs across borders. In Germany, I saw children raised with discipline and structure, values that follow them into workplaces where order and hierarchy are deeply respected. In England, intellect and heritage shape identity, with education as both ladder and legacy. In the Netherlands, the imprint is different: Dutch children are raised with a merchant's mindset — practical, egalitarian, encouraged to learn by doing, to weigh choices with pragmatism more than ideology.

Amsterdam itself has taught me contrasts too. Outsiders imagine it as a city of red lights and endless freedom, but in our corner of *de Jordaan** it feels more like a village. Neighbours nod as they pass on bicycles, grandmothers scold children for mischief, families gather at home for birthdays marked by modest rituals — a five-year-old invites five friends, a six-year-old six. Frugality is disguised as warmth, and extravagance is frowned upon.

In Malaysia, where I was raised, success today is more often displayed through logos, cars, and schools. Here, pride is quieter: not in what you show, but in how you live. Neither is better or worse. Each reflects what its people have been taught to hold sacred.

Sometimes, when I look at Camilla and Isabel, I see these contrasts shining through them — the Dutch openness, the Malay

* *De Jordaan* — once a working-class district of Amsterdam, now a neighbourhood with a village-like spirit, where everyday life carries a sense of community.

tenderness, the French lyricism. They are mosaics, alive with fragments that might not match, but together, they catch the light in ways I could never have planned.

Tunggulah Nanti

My ancestors had a phrase for patience: *tunggulah nanti* — wait, and you will see. It was never spoken as a suggestion, but as a command. A reminder that life is not to be rushed, that time itself will reveal what is meant to unfold.

I heard it in my grandmother's kitchen, between the rolling of spices and the chorus of aunties talking over each other. I heard it in my mother's voice when she was displeased with me, sharp with prophecy: *Tunggulah nanti!*[*] Wait until you are a mother. Wait until you feel what I have felt. It was a phrase that carried both wisdom and warning, as if my own pain would one day vindicate hers.

Across cultures, mothers echo the phrases of their foremothers, passing them down like heirlooms — some wrapped in tenderness, others edged like blades. What sounds like patience is sometimes also a curse, a wish that the daughter will be pierced by the same sorrow, so she will finally understand.

This is the double edge of inheritance. We receive blessings, but also burdens; resilience, but also unfinished grief. And when we migrate, we do not leave these legacies at the border. We carry them folded into our bodies, our silences, our speech.

To marry across cultures is not just to blend cuisines or customs. It is to braid together the transmissions[†] of two families, two histories, two shadows. The blessings multiply, but so do the burdens. What was once a single thread becomes a tapestry of

---

* *Tunggulah nanti* — Malay for "wait, later" or "just wait and see." Often spoken as both prophecy and warning, especially from mothers to daughters.

† *Intergenerational transmission* — psychologists describe how behaviours, beliefs, and even traumas are unconsciously passed down through families, replayed until someone interrupts the cycle.

tangled lines, crossing and knotting in ways no one could have predicted.

I know this in my own life. The Malay patience that steadied me also made me swallow words I should have spoken. The inherited deference that carried dignity also carried shame. And still, I hear my mother in my voice — certain phrases slipping out before I can catch them, echoes of a woman whose own mother spoke the same way. My husband too carries his mother in him, her tones and gestures surfacing in ways that distance has not erased.

We do not escape these imprints; they live in us like the architecture of instinct. But repetition does not mean replication. Kierkegaard called repetition the way life teaches us; Deleuze wrote that repetition always produces difference*. Perhaps this is what marriage and parenting reveal: the same notes, played in another key.

Migration complicates it further. Malay patience, French lyricism, Dutch pragmatism, English reserve — each pattern lives in me now, sometimes clashing, sometimes harmonising. Change is possible, but never absolute. What matters is how we respond: which threads we choose to keep, which knots we learn to loosen, and which burdens we allow to end with us.

Perhaps *tunggulah nanti* means not only to wait for life to unfold, but to wait for ourselves to grow ready. Patience is not passivity; it is the tending of a garden, knowing which seeds to sow, which weeds to pull, which roots to let deepen unseen.

And perhaps that is the truest meaning of *tunggulah nanti*: not a command, not a curse, but an invitation. To wait with openness.

To trust that even what feels unfinished can carry us forward.

Not everything needs to be resolved in our lifetime.

Some burdens will soften on their own.

Some blessings will bloom in ways we cannot yet imagine.

---

* *Repetition in philosophy* — Kierkegaard saw repetition as life's way of teaching; Deleuze argued repetition always creates difference, never perfect sameness.

And maybe what we leave our daughters is not a perfect inheritance, but the space to weave their own.

The Blue Ocean

When Isabel was born, I thought I had already learned how to mother. Camilla had taught me that motherhood was not compartmentalised but woven into everything: work, faith, love, migration. I thought the map of those lessons would guide me again. But Isabel arrived with her own geography, one I had never seen before.

Her diagnosis, a rare neurological condition, tore up the map I thought I had. Suddenly there were no landmarks, no signposts, only questions. Doctors gave us medical language, but it was not the same as direction. What I had was a child whose milestones came slowly, whose words arrived as fragile mosaics, and then slipped away altogether. What I had was love, fierce and unmeasured, trying to stretch itself across uncertainty.

The grief came in waves, uninvited and unpredictable. It was not always in the big moments, but in the smallest: the pause when another mother spoke of milestones, the silence when forms asked for abilities Isabel did not have, the sting of well-meant comparisons. My body carried the weight of it, stuck in my chest, fatigue in my limbs. Gazillion thoughts racing in my mind.

I searched for ways to steady myself: tending to breath, leaning into rituals, finding pockets of stillness where I could. I travelled far, even to an ashram in Lakshman Jhula at the foot of the Himalayas, hoping distance might reveal direction. But what I found was clarity, and the sharp contours of the absence of the map. It did not appear. What emerged instead was the deep ache itself, insisting to be released.

Sometimes renewal felt like demolition. I did not know how to integrate the new identity also as the mother of a special needs child and rare disease advocate. The ground kept shifting, and my identity with it. And yet, something was forming in that rubble.

Isabel herself was my teacher. Her smile, her gaze, her stubborn joy taught me that presence mattered more than progress, that life could still be whole without fitting any chart.

Scientists call this *adaptive expertise*[*] — the ability to navigate terrain with no rules, not by repeating the old, but by inventing the new. It is less about mastery than flexibility. That, I realised, is what Isabel was teaching me: not how to follow the map, but how to draw one slowly, with patience and imagination, as we went.

Science tells us that when we stand before situations with no precedent, the brain cannot lean on its usual shortcuts of memory or experience. Instead, it turns to intuition[†], that quiet synthesis of fragments we cannot name. Entrepreneurs speak of *blue oceans*[‡], vast spaces without markers, where you must invent as you go. Parenting Isabel felt like that. I was not following a map but sensing a horizon, one step at a time, learning to trust that not-knowing could itself be a form of wisdom.

Modern life has trained us to prize certainty. We build systems, write manuals, collect data. We tell ourselves that if we plan carefully enough, we can control the outcome. But intuition is the older map — one humanity relied on long before charts or signposts. It guided sailors across unmarked seas, traders through deserts, mothers through childbirth without instruction. It is the quiet pulse beneath thought, a knowing that does not always announce its reasons.

Psychologists tell the story of a firefighter[§] who once pulled

---

* *Adaptive expertise* — a kind of flexible intelligence that thrives in new or unpredictable situations; rather than relying on fixed rules, it creates fresh approaches. Essential when the map does not exist.

† *Intuition* — the brain's rapid, unconscious synthesis of subtle cues and past experiences, allowing us to act when logic has no precedent.

‡ *Blue oceans* — a business metaphor for uncharted territory, where competition is irrelevant and new possibilities must be imagined.

§ Psychologist Gary Klein, who studied decision-making in high-stakes environments, often cites a case of a firefighter who pulled his crew from a house fire seconds before the floor collapsed. He couldn't explain why at the time — only later did he realise his body had registered subtle cues. Klein used this to show that

his crew from what seemed like a routine blaze. Moments later, the floor collapsed. He could not explain why he had acted — only later did he realise his body had registered details his mind had not. This is how intuition works: a knowing before we can name it.

Crossing borders demanded that I return to this lost skill. There was no guidebook for raising Isabel, no cultural script to follow, no wisdom handed down that matched the terrain I now walked. Intuition became the compass. It tells me when to pause, when to push, when to ask for help. It stitched together fragments of experience into direction. It was not always right, but it was alive — and in moments when the ground disappeared beneath me, it showed up more than cognitive intelligence.

I realised that renewal is not a one-time event but a daily practice. Some days it meant walking until the weight lifted. Some days it meant sitting in the dark until tears ran their course. Some days it meant laughing with Camilla at the dinner table, letting light in through the cracks. And some days, it meant simply surviving, trusting that even survival is a kind of prayer.

The truth is, none of us are given a complete map. We inherit fragments from our families, instructions from our cultures, lessons from our faiths. But sooner or later, life tears those papers up and hands us a blank page.

To live without a map is terrifying, but it is also where reinvention begins. Isabel, without words, showed me that. My daughters remind me daily that love itself is a compass, more reliable than any chart.

We like to believe that life comes with a map. We write frameworks, invent formulas, and fill shelves with guidebooks that promise to chart the way. And perhaps this is our ancient brain at work, doing what it has always done: tracing the footsteps of our ancestors, learning from the past to protect the future. It is remarkable that we can inherit wisdom like this.

---

intuition is not guesswork but expertise stored in the body, surfacing when reason has no time to catch up.

But life is never only about following the footsteps. It is also about stepping into places no one has charted yet. Sometimes it is better to close the manual, forget the internet tabs, and wander a little — the way our ancestors once did when they crossed oceans, carrying only instinct and courage. Look how far we've come, and they did not even have Google map.

The little girl with the pencil pouch with the red double decker bus still swims with me in the blue ocean, teaching me that even across borders and losses, wonder and courage are enough to draw the path as I go.

Part 3: THE RETURN

The Integration
The Presence
The Continuance

Chapter 9

New Frequency

The Birth of Awareness

There is a moment in every journey of becoming, a moment so subtle it can almost be missed, yet unmistakable when it arrives. Friction no longer feels like resistance. It becomes revelation.

You have changed.

What once fit no longer does. Laughter rings shallow. Rituals feel rehearsed. Conversations that once flowed now feel heavy. The frequency has shifted, and your body knows it before your mind does.

Friction arrives first as discomfort: a heaviness after familiar gatherings, the fatigue of explaining yourself, the subtle ways you shrink or stretch to stay in tune with those around you. Sometimes it is just a word that lands sharp in your gut, a silence that feels punishing, a tradition that once wrapped you in tenderness but now pierces.

This ache is different from the grief of departure. That grief was about what was taken from you. This grief is about what you consciously choose to release. It is not exile but discernment. Not abandonment but realignment.

Here self-awareness becomes the hinge. It is the mirror that shows you when you have outgrown an old rhythm. Without it, you might mistake the ache for failure, or the friction for a flaw. With it, you begin to see that the discomfort is not an enemy but an invitation. Awareness transforms sorrow into agency, and pain into a compass pointing you toward a truer alignment.

Psychology calls this a threshold of growth. Jung called it *individuation*[*] — the lifelong process of becoming who you are, not who others expect you to be. Maslow placed self-awareness at the heart of *self-actualisation*[†], the highest need of all. Neuroscience[‡], too, speaks of the same truth: that simply noticing our patterns reshapes the brain, softening old reflexes and opening doors to new ways of being.

For me, this mirror only became clear later in life. Until then, I moved through life propelled by instinct and hunger, ambition carrying me from one table to the next, reinvention stitched together by necessity. I was changing all along, but I did not see myself changing.

It was slightly before I reached forty that awareness came with unmistakable force. I could suddenly look back and trace the arc: the teenager who left Malaysia because at seven she was inspired by the red double decker bus on her pencil case, the woman who built businesses across continents, the mother whose body became a home for others. I had been so busy becoming that I had not paused to notice what I had become.

Science offers one explanation. Self-awareness is not fully formed in youth; it matures as the brain itself matures. The prefrontal cortex — the region responsible for reflection and integration — continues developing into our twenties and strengthens

---

* *Individuation (Jung)* — the lifelong unfolding of becoming your authentic self, distinct from the roles others assign.

† *Self-actualisation (Maslow)* — awareness as the gateway to living fully, with creativity, purpose, and freedom.

‡ *Neuroplasticity* — the brain's ability to rewire itself when we notice and choose differently; awareness as biology's poetry.

with age. By midlife, its networks are more intricately connected, allowing us to hold complexity and see patterns across time. The amygdala, once quick to flare in youth, begins to calm. Emotional reactivity softens, leaving space for perspective.

This is what some call the stage of integration*. We are no longer driven only by novelty or survival. Memory and identity begin to weave themselves into a coherent story. Awareness sharpens here not as ornament, but as necessity. It is the mind's own evolution asking us to live more deliberately.

In many cultures, age has always been seen not as decline but as a crown. In traditional Malay society, elders were not only respected but entrusted as *penghulu*† — leaders of villages whose authority came not from wealth or force but from years lived, stories carried, and wisdom distilled through experience. Age itself was a credential. To be older was to have endured, to have witnessed, to have integrated life into layers of perspective.

And yet, in many modern societies, the wisdom of elders is often overlooked. There is a kind of arrogance in youth that assumes experience is outdated, especially in an age when technology makes information instantly accessible. Knowledge is now at everyone's fingertips, searchable in seconds, and so the carriers of knowledge — the older ones who once held it as treasure — are sometimes dismissed as irrelevant.

But information is not the same as wisdom. Technology can alter the pace of our days, streamline our tasks, even simulate forms of intelligence. What it cannot replicate is the slow accumulation of understanding that comes only through living: through grief endured, mistakes made, love tested, and resilience shaped across decades.

Perhaps the true offering of age is not efficiency but depth.

---

* *Stage of integration* — midlife as a developmental turning point where memory, identity, and perspective weave into a coherent whole.

† *Penghulu* — in traditional Malay society, the village elder whose authority rested on wisdom, endurance, and the trust of the community.

Where technology accelerates, elders remind us to pause. Where artificial intelligence delivers answers, elders embody the questions that matter. In a world chasing speed, the experience of being fully human remains the one inheritance only age can carry.

This reverence echoes what psychology now calls the stage of integration. When you have crossed borders, weathered changes, and gathered identities across different seasons, you begin to hold not only your own story but the stories of those who came before you. You become, in a sense, a living archive — one who carries the fragments of many places, many selves, and makes them whole.

And so it was with me. After forty, I began to feel the fractures and shifts more distinctly. I noticed when I was bending out of tune, when a conversation drained instead of nourished, when a ritual no longer carried the tenderness it once did. Self-awareness became less an idea and more a current in my body — the reminder that the deepest act of evolution is not only to change, but to witness yourself changing.

One of the clearest signs that awareness is alive within us is the ability to release what no longer serves. This does not always arrive as grand decisions or dramatic partings, but as the steady pruning of what no longer resonates, what no longer brings vitality or joy.

To choose carefully what to carry forward is not rejection but refinement — the wisdom of knowing that life has seasons, and that every ending creates the ground for new beginnings.

Letting go becomes less about loss and more about alignment. It is the evidence that awareness is doing its work, shaping us into people who do not cling out of fear but choose with intention.

There is a tenderness in this kind of loss. Once, falling away felt like abandonment — by others, by life, by the old self.

Now it feels like falling inward. It feels sore, even if gentle. Like a leaf letting go of its branch at the first wind of autumn in the Netherlands. Not anger, not drama, just the separation of what no longer resonates.

The Rainforest as My Teacher

When I search for a language beyond psychology or science, I return to the rainforest* of my childhood land. Its wisdom is etched into my bones.

In the heart of the jungle, every ending carries the seed of a beginning. A fallen leaf is not wasted but becomes nourishment for the soil below. What looks like decay is renewal: fungi feeding on what has been shed, insects making homes of what is broken, seedlings rising from what no longer stands.

Nothing is discarded. Everything is transformed. Growth in the forest is never a straight line — it spirals, improvises, and responds to change.

As a young child, I was afraid of the rainforest — the *hutan*† that loomed just beyond the familiar edges of my Kuala Lumpur life. I trembled at the thought of leeches clinging to my skin or snakes sliding silently in the undergrowth.

I remember it most vividly after rain, when the boarding school I attended seemed to dissolve into the thick chorus of cicadas and the earth steamed as though the ground itself was breathing. I trembled at the thought of leeches clinging to my skin or snakes sliding silently in the undergrowth.

This fear was not only mine. In Malay heritage, the forest was never seen as empty. It was alive with other beings — guardians, spirits, unseen presences who dwelled alongside us. Children were taught never to trespass lightly, to whisper permission from the *'datok and nenek'*‡ of the forest, the unseen elders said to live among the trees. The *hutan* was both provider and mystery, a

---

* *The Malaysian rainforest* is among the world's oldest, over 130 million years, and home to countless species. Often called the lungs of the earth, it regulates climate and holds immense biodiversity.

† *Hutan* means forest in Malay, carrying both ecological and spiritual weight.

‡ *Datok* (grandfather) and *nenek* (grandmother) are names given to the unseen guardians of the forest in Malay cosmology, honoured before entering as a gesture of respect.

place of medicine and sustenance, but also of caution, reverence, and respect.

Years later, seeing the rainforest on European screens, I was startled to find the old fear replaced by longing. The damp scent of earth that once unsettled me now felt like home. The hum of cicadas was no longer warning, but music. What once frightened me had become anchor, a reminder not only of Malaysia's inheritance but of the lungs of the earth — a cathedral where every fall is gathered, every breath shared.

The rainforest teaches by example. It does not hurry, it does not cling. It transforms. It shows us that nothing is wasted, that endings are not erasure but renewal.

Neuroscience echoes this truth. The brain, like the forest, thrives on pruning and renewal. Connections that no longer serve are pared away, creating space for stronger ones to grow. Each release makes room for new vitality.

And so too with us. A friendship that ends may compost into clarity. A role we outgrow may become the fertile ground of another beginning. Loss itself may root tenderness we never knew we carried.

To live with awareness is to stand inside our own rainforest. To notice which parts of us are blooming, which are ready to be pruned, which are quietly transforming beneath the surface. The forest reminds us that release is not failure but continuity, and that even the hardest fall may one day return, transformed.

What you release will feed the future you cannot yet see.

A Different Story

When Isabel's rare condition entered our lives, the map of everything shifted. Connections that once felt central quietly faded, like rivers sinking into new ground. Some friendships could not follow us into this altered landscape. Their absence carried no anger, only the sadness of paths that diverged.

And yet, in the space grief carved out, a new community appeared — one I would never have known without her.

In Amsterdam, beneath the arches of the train tracks near Central Station, I found *A Different Story*, a circle created by Sarah Rose LaPham, a fellow migrant. Parents gathered there from Malaysia, Chile, the Netherlands, Israel, France, the US. The scent of coffee with oat milk mingled with *krentebollen*[*] and biscuits on the table. Trains rumbled overhead. Laughter and tears sat side by side.

Here, I learned the language of "living loss"[†] — Dr. Pauline Boss's phrase for the grief of loving someone who is alive, while mourning the future you once imagined for them. Each missed milestone, each diagnosis, became a double sorrow: for Isabel's struggle and for the parallel life that slipped further from reach.

This world is invisible to many, sometimes misunderstood, often judged. Some days, unbearably lonely. But here, there was no need to explain. No need to hide exhaustion or mask disappointment. We cried and laughed, confessed our anger, swapped stories of sleepless nights and small victories. We carried one another in the dark.

These friendships endure, not because they are light, but because they honour the shadow. They remind me that beauty does not live only in joy, but in the ways we help each other bear what is unbearable.

Some connections die their natural death; some drift quietly into memory. But in this cocoon, I have been reminded again and again that the soul is nourished not by numbers, but by presence. By those rare companions who choose to stay.

Without communities like this, the work of grieving and healing would feel impossible. But in the burn and glow of shared

---

* *Krentebollen* — Dutch currant buns, lightly sweet and chewy, often eaten with butter. A staple of school lunches and coffee breaks.

† *Living loss* — Concept coined by Dr. Pauline Boss to describe grief when a loved one is physically present but the imagined future with them is lost.

witness, I have learned what Viktor Frankl* once wrote: *"What is to give light must endure burning."*

We become light for each other not in spite of struggle, but because of it.

Perhaps you, too, know the unexpected beauty that comes from carrying one another through the dark.

Amanah

Ancient wisdom tells us that change is not chaos but law. Every ease carries its hardship, every hardship its ease. The Qur'an echoes this mercy in Surah Al-Inshirah: *fa inna ma'al usri yusra, inna ma'al usri yusra* — with difficulty comes relief, with difficulty comes relief. Nature teaches the same truth: winter makes spring possible; sorrow becomes the soil for new joy.

So too with human connection. Some people remain in harmony with us across decades, like my school friends Wa, Julie, and Yana, whose truths still resonate with mine after more than forty years. Others drift, even after years of trying to retune ourselves to the old song. And then the lesson arrives: some bonds are meant for a season, not a lifetime.

Letting go is not the absence of love, but its deepest form. Prophets and sages have spoken of patience, of *amanah*† — life as a sacred trust, to be tended and returned. They remind us that what we release is not wasted, but will return in another form, sometimes here, sometimes in the life to come.

With self-awareness comes a deeper responsibility. To see my own journey clearly, with its choices and consequences, is not only a gift but a duty. Awareness is not meant to end in the self. It

---

* *Viktor Frankl* — Austrian psychiatrist and Holocaust survivor, who wrote *Man's Search for Meaning*. His line "What is to give light must endure burning" is a touchstone for finding purpose in suffering.

† *Amanah* — In Islamic faith and Malay tradition means sacred trust or responsibility. Life itself is considered an *amanah*, to be safeguarded with care and integrity.

asks us to turn what we have endured — even the mistakes, even the pain — into something useful for others.

In Malay Muslim tradition, this is *amanah*: a trust placed in our hands, to be lived with integrity and offered back with care. Life itself is an *amanah*, and Malay culture teaches that every promise, every role, every relationship is bound by it. Yet this truth is not ours alone. Other cultures, too, carry their own words for this trust. The essence is the same: to live with honour is to live not only for oneself, but for the web of others we touch.

Self-awareness, then, is never only a mirror. It is a covenant — the reminder that the lessons of our lives are not ours to hoard, but to share. To integrate awareness with *amanah* is to recognise that belonging is not just a gift we receive, but also a responsibility we carry.

For those of us who live across borders, the meaning of this trust deepens. Every migration, every threshold crossed, every identity stretched across languages and landscapes becomes part of what we are responsible for.

Belonging is not only about finding safety; it is also about what we give back. The stories we inherit, the lessons we gather, the fractures we mend — all of it becomes an offering, a way of returning what has carried us.

This is the paradox of change: to belong everywhere and nowhere, and yet to know that our lives still bear responsibility. Self-belonging is not selfishness. It is the ground from which we can give. To live with *amanah* is to honour what has shaped us and to leave something of worth for those who will come after us.

Consensus ad Idem

What ancient traditions intuited, modern science now measures: everything vibrates. Every atom, every cell, every breath carries a rhythm.

When two systems align, they resonate. When they clash, dissonance rises like static*.

Our bodies are instruments too. Sit with someone calm, and your breath steadies. Stand near someone anxious, and your pulse begins to race. From birth, we learn this synchrony — an infant soothed by the cadence of a mother's voice, a child steadied by a father's arms. Later, it is a friend whose laugh softens the day, or a community whose presence lowers the weight in your chest.

Even the brain echoes what surrounds it. Mirror neurons† fire when we see another smile, stumble, or cry, as if the moment were happening inside us. Joy spreads. Despair too. We are wired to tune in to one another.

This is why connection matters. Every friendship, every gathering, every bond is not only social but biological. Some companions steady our heartbeat. Others keep us braced. And the choice of who surrounds us becomes, quite literally, a matter of survival.

For those of us who move across borders, this truth becomes even sharper. Home is not only the passport we carry but the frequencies we keep. A single friendship can anchor us across oceans; a new bond can make foreign soil feel like ground.

I think of Bea Salomma, a Polish friend I always enjoy meeting up with in Amsterdam. We have seen each other only a handful of times, yet our first conversation stretched for hours as if time bent to make room. We share no culture, no history, no particular similarity — but there was a kind of *consensus ad idem*‡ between us, a meeting of minds that needed no blueprint. Not because we are the same, but because we both choose to listen, to laugh, to hold space for difference.

Friendships are frequencies we return to again and again.

---

* *Law of Vibration*: Ancient Hermetic thought, echoed in Hindu *spanda* and Taoist *qi*, and mirrored in physics, teaches that all life vibrates in constant motion.

† *Mirror neurons:* Discovered in the 1990s, these brain cells show how we echo each other's emotions and actions — a biological basis for empathy.

‡ *Consensus ad idem*: A Latin phrase meaning "meeting of minds," often used in law, here describing the harmony between lives that choose to meet.

Some endure for decades, adapting as we do. Others fade quietly, their melody no longer ours. To honour these shifts is to recognise that connection itself is alive — changing, evolving, always in motion.

Physics, biology, psychology — they all whisper the same truth: nothing rests, everything moves. Every bond is a field of resonance. Some notes last a lifetime. Others end after a single season. But all leave their tone within us.

Perhaps this is what it means to belong inside change: to know that even as people come and go, each has left their note for our own jazz ensemble.

The Tender Work of Realignment

Realignment is rarely dramatic. It unfolds in the ordinary adjustments a new place demands: the pace of mornings, the shape of meals, the way people measure time.

In Germany, trains and timetables ruled the day, demanding precision. In France, time slowed at the table, meals stretching into conversations that carried through the night. In the Netherlands, bluntness was honesty, and even the smallest interactions echoed with directness.

For me, realignment was always a negotiation: how to soften the edges of my difference without dissolving my uniqueness. In England, I learned that English was not only a language but a code — sentences saying one thing while implying another. Once I caught the rhythm, I found my place. In Germany, clarity itself was kindness; rules made it easy to know where I stood. The Netherlands brought another kind of ease: directness that never demanded conformity, only civility. Beneath its liberal freedoms ran a strong current of restraint.

What proved more difficult was not Europe, but home. Returning to Malaysia after thirty years abroad, I found myself strangely out of step. My body was Malay and Muslim, but my life had stretched beyond those borders. Without the *hijab**, I stood out — unless I retreated into neighbourhoods where difference was tolerated. In affluent † Kuala Lumpur suburbs, my unbranded clothes felt almost defiant in seas of designer labels. Abroad, realignment felt natural. At home, it sometimes felt impossible.

The same was true in my work. As an entrepreneur, I found it easier to collaborate with strangers from faraway countries than with my own. Among Malaysians, I often met a different yardstick. Nationalism and stricter forms of Islam painted me as too Western or not Muslim enough to be befriended by some. It is the absurdity of belonging: to be embraced abroad while questioned at home.

Perhaps this is the hardest paradox of realignment. We expect foreign soil to ask something of us — new codes, new rhythms, new adjustments. But home, we imagine, should ask nothing at all. And yet it is often the place where the demand to conform presses the heaviest.

Abroad, I can stand out and still belong. At home, standing out can feel like disqualification.

Realignment, then, is not simply about geography. It is about living in the tension between who we have become and what others expect us to be.

Sometimes it is easy, even effortless. Sometimes it aches. But across every border, the work is the same: to remain whole while learning, again and again, how to move differently in the world.

---

* *Hijab*: In Islamic tradition, hijab refers both to modest dress (most often a headscarf) and to the principle of modesty more broadly. In Malaysia today, it carries layers of meaning — faith, identity, family tradition, and, increasingly, fashion.

† *Bangsar, Kiara, Ampang, TTDI and Damansar***a**: Affluent neighbourhoods in Kuala Lumpur, associated with prestige, international schools, and designer labels — markers of belonging in contemporary Malaysia.

Lessons from My Long Table

My table is Malay in its welcome: always set for one more, food never measured, portions always generous. Wherever I am, I invite company to linger, to toast each arrival, to let conversation meander into the night. In London, I learned the quiet joy of clearing the table myself, stretching the pleasure of cooking beyond the meal.

Some friends and family will always have a seat, even if they do not visit often. Loyalty, for me, is memory. I remember Susi and Bob in London, who fed me when I was hungry and checked on me when the world felt wide and empty. From them I learned that hospitality is not transaction but gift.

Yet loyalty is also impermanence. Some guests come and go, the chairs shift, the table changes shape. Still, the root remains: the Malay generosity that remembers even where you fell, and even more, the places you found joy.

Friendships are seasons. Some arrive like spring, riotous and bright. Others settle like autumn, golden and quiet. Family can be stormy or steadfast, and sometimes you must step outside to breathe. But the root of kindness, loyalty, and care endures, even as geographies and circumstances change.

The Malays call this *jodoh*[*] — the mysterious timing that brings people together and lets them part. It is not possession, not permanence, but the recognition that encounters come when they are meant to. Some leave quietly, others with ceremony, but each leaves an imprint. Goodbyes have taught me as much as the meals themselves. In French we say *au revoir* — until we see each other again. In Dutch, *dag* — both greeting and parting. In Malay, *selamat jalan* — may your journey be safe. Every language encodes the same truth: farewells carry blessing as much as loss.

---

* *Jodoh:* In Malay culture, *jodoh* means destined encounters — meetings or partings that unfold with their own timing. Not possession, but recognition that certain people cross our path when they are meant to.

The long table has also taught me heartbreak and boundaries. One of my hardest lessons came with a girlfriend. I gave her loyalty, believing it could bridge any difference. I helped, I stood by her, I opened my home and my heart. But with the smallest conflict, everything vanished. For her, an argument was an ending. For me, it was just another wave to ride together. That rupture revealed something I had not seen: for some, loyalty is measured by harmony, not endurance.

We are shaped both by who sits across from us and by who leaves. Marina Abramović captured this truth in her performance *The Artist Is Present**: for 700 hours she sat in silence across from strangers, holding their gaze. Some wept, some laughed, some simply breathed more deeply. Presence alone was transformative.

Loss teaches us too. Neuroscience shows that rupture† can harden us or open us. Each disappointment becomes a choice: to build walls, or to learn the art of boundaries — lines drawn not in anger but in wisdom.

This lesson has returned most often with my mother. Her love, fierce as it is, sometimes carries expectations that drain more than they give. She longs for me to remain the child who reflects her belonging. From her, I have learned that boundaries can be a gift to both giver and receiver. Sometimes the greatest act of loyalty is to care for myself, to keep my spirit whole enough to offer warmth freely, not out of duty.

Sometimes I leave a seat empty — for the one who is gone, the friend yet to come, or the part of myself still returning. The empty chair is not only absence, but hope: grief made gentle, space for possibility.

And in this shifting world, the table itself has changed shape.

* *Marina Abramović, The Artist Is Present* (2010): A performance at MoMA where Abramović sat silently across from strangers for over 700 hours. The work revealed how simple presence can create profound connection.

† *Rupture and Repair*: Developmental psychology shows that resilience in relationships is built not by perfection but by cycles of rupture and repair. These moments teach trust, discernment, and the capacity to love with boundaries.

Some days it is digital, lit by screens, faces scattered across time zones. Hospitality grows more complex; we must decide not only who to welcome, but how much of ourselves we can truly give. Boundaries are not barriers but gentle lines, protecting the root of generosity so it can remain sincere, not depleted.

Perhaps this is the truest test of loyalty now: to know when to extend a hand, when to hold space, and when to keep a seat empty for our own quiet returning.

The table is not infinite, though the world may try to make it so. I remind myself of three simple things: the courage to begin again, the memory of kindness, and the ability to sit in stillness with myself. These will never be outgrown, no matter how long the table stretches.

Sometimes wood, sometimes pixels, sometimes memory — the table holds the laughter of friends, the silences of those who have gone, the hope of those yet to arrive. In the end, it is not its fullness but the intention behind each seat that matters.

The long table is not only where we gather others. It is where we learn to gather ourselves.

The Spiral of Becoming

Growing in the tropics, I would play in the garden of our home, crouching low to search for centipedes. I would prod them gently with a stick, and watch with delight as they curled in on themselves — as if the whole world could be held in their coiled bodies. Young Nina found it endlessly amusing — the tiny creature folding into a spiral, as if the whole world could be held in its coiled body.

Later I learned that this shape — the spiral — is one of nature's oldest signatures. It curves through galaxies and seashells, unfurls in the fronds of ferns, and even guides the pattern of storms. The mathematicians call it the Fibonacci spiral*, a rhythm of growth

* *Fibonacci Spiral:* A natural pattern linked to the golden ratio, appearing in

that repeats across scales. It is etched in our DNA, in the ridges of our fingerprints, in the iris of every eye. And before we ever opened those eyes, each of us rested in the womb in that same spiral shape — curled, protected, waiting for life to unfold.

The rainforest knows this language too. Beneath its canopy, roots are laced together through fungal threads — the 'wood-wide web'* — carrying food, messages, and warnings across species and generations. The oldest "mother trees" share their strength with seedlings hidden from the sun, keeping them alive until they can stand on their own. The forest survives not because every tree stands alone, but because its roots are intertwined.

So it is with us. Living across cultures, moving through change, I have learned that we too are sustained by unseen webs: the kindness of strangers, the loyalty of friends, the memory of those who once sat at our tables. Some ties loosen, others are cut, yet the root system of belonging remains. What falls away does not vanish but becomes nourishment for what is yet to grow.

To live within the spiral is to trust that each loss, each reunion, each migration enlarges us. We cannot freeze the moment of togetherness any more than we can stop the turning of seasons. People arrive and depart, identities stretch and reshape, stories open and close. The work is not to resist the spiral, but to walk it with grace — returning, revisiting, relearning, always at a deeper layer than before.

This is the paradox of becoming. Our lives expand as much through rupture as through repair, through solitude as through company.

The web beneath us does not vanish when branches break

---

galaxies, seashells, storms, sunflowers, DNA, fingerprints, and the iris of the eye — reminders that life grows through expansion and return, never in straight lines.

* *Wood-Wide Web:* The underground fungal network that connects trees, allowing them to share nutrients and signals. "Mother trees" feed and protect seedlings through these threads, showing that resilience in nature is communal, not solitary.

above. It waits quietly, reminding us that no fall is final, and no renewal is without memory.

To live as spiral is to accept belonging as layered, unfinished, alive. It is not a permanent home but a rhythm of roots and renewal, a pattern written into galaxies and seashells, into DNA and fingerprints, into the wombs that once held us, into the marrow of our becoming.

And sometimes I think back to the little girl in the garden, watching a centipede curl into itself. What she saw as play was, perhaps, her first lesson in the shape of life: that everything folds, returns, and expands again. That even the smallest spiral can hold the secret of becoming.

Chapter 10

Living by Design

Ma Empty Chair

After the falling away, after the spirals of release and rupture, there is a pause.

A stillness.

The table is not crowded anymore. A chair sits empty.

In that space, something shifts. What once felt like absence begins to feel like possibility.

The empty chair is not only loss; it is invitation. A clearing. The spaciousness that comes after pruning, the moment when you can ask quietly: *Who do I want beside me now?*

I have come to see that this emptiness is not a void to be feared, but a kind of architecture.

In Malay we say: *kosong* — empty, but also open, uncluttered, waiting.

In Arabic, *firaagh* carries the same double edge: emptiness as both ache and opening.

The empty chair is the jet lag in my heart.

When I finish work and call home, it is already midnight in Malaysia. When I wake, the voices I long for are already deep in their day. I spend mornings replying to yesterday, evenings trying to catch tomorrow. I am always just out of step — present everywhere, but never quite in sync. The chair is not empty because there is no love, but because time itself is misaligned.

Other times, the empty chair reveals itself in the crowded room. Conferences, parties, even family gatherings — many voices, much laughter, yet not the one presence that makes me feel safe enough to exhale.

These days, I move between communities, networks, and circles where there is always someone to talk to, always a crowd to mingle with. But friendship — the kind that steadies you — takes time. And so, even while busy, even while surrounded, loneliness lingers quietly. Many migrants know too well: the ache of being full of people, yet still feeling the weight of an empty chair.

The Japanese call this space *ma* — the silence between notes in music, the pause between breaths, the blankness around a brushstroke in calligraphy. Not absence, but presence. Without it, nothing can breathe.

The empty chair at the table is its own *ma* — a reminder that not every seat needs to be filled for the gathering to be whole.

As children, belonging is given to us. Family, neighbours, classmates — chairs already arranged by birth and geography. But adulthood is different. Belonging is no longer coincidence; it is design. The table does not set itself. We choose who sits beside us, whose voices shape us, whose presence steadies or unsettles our hearts.

This is the work of belonging by intention: to see emptiness not as punishment, but as possibility. To let the empty chair remind us that absence, too, can be beautiful.

Resonance

It was only after the table grew emptier that I realised its emptiness was a gift.

Once, friendship was proximity.

The girl who borrowed your school uniform.

The intern who shared your sense of humour.

A business contact who became a confidant, carrying your secrets.

But the migrant's heart — shaped by airports and farewells — learns this truth: belonging, as you grow, becomes less about geography and more about resonance.

I think back to my years in London, and later in Gütersloh — young, ambitious, foreign, desperate to prove that I deserved my place in the world. My workdays stretched long into the night, glass towers shimmering with ambition, yet often more isolating than inspiring. In those early years, I welcomed almost anyone who seemed to be moving in the same direction, mistaking proximity for resonance*.

It is easy to do, especially when you live abroad. New postings, new cities, new flats — there are always acquaintances, dinner parties, and colleagues willing to fill the hours. For a while, it feels like belonging. But after the laughter fades and the wine glasses are cleared, you realise how rare it is to find the friend who stays, the one who holds your story across years and continents. Busyness can fill the room, but only resonance fills the heart.

Now, I no longer crave a crowd. I seek frequency — not the loudest, but the most attuned. The ones whose laughter rings true, whose silence feels safe, whose presence is a soft place to land.

Rumi once wrote: *"Set your life on fire. Seek those who fan your flames."*† It is not enough for someone to simply sit beside you; their energy must lift you, kindle something alive within.

Mardi has always lived in my heart. We met as university students, sharing a flat and the awkward intimacies of young adulthood — the split rent, the mismatched dishes, the long nights of ramen and possibility. Life scattered us across continents, but each time we found our way back, the resonance was immediate,

---

* *Proximity ≠ resonance:* busyness and acquaintances may fill the table, but only true friends fill the heart.

† *Rumi:* Fire as metaphor — friendship as kindling for the soul.

as if no time had passed. Deep friendships are like that — not erased by distance, only resting, waiting for a laugh or a story to wake them.

Through Mardi, I came to know Ali, his Russian partner. With him, too, a bond grew — different, but just as steady. Ours was not the easy continuity of old history, but the immediate recognition of kindred rhythm. The architecture of my belonging widened to hold them both — two friendships distinct, yet equally enduring, because each was built on the same deeper frequency: the rare courage to see each other fully, and to stay.

Aristotle once described such bonds as "a single soul dwelling in two bodies." A true friend is like a polished mirror — reflecting not only what is bright in us, but also what is tender, unfinished, luminous.

This is why, for the soul in motion, gathering bodies around a table is no longer enough.

Now, I choose to gather those who bring light — those who remind me who I am, and who I wish to be. Those who look into the cracks and do not turn away, but gently say: *You are more than your weakness. I still see your fire.*

This is the sacred shift: from inherited community to chosen family. To gather not just those who are near, but those who meet you at the right frequency — those who fan your spirit's flame, and call you quietly home to yourself.

In the architecture of your own becoming, who will you choose to let in and fill that empty chair?

The Mechanics of Connections

There is a quiet revolution that happens in the body when you are truly seen — not just tolerated, but cherished.

When you stand in the light of a friend who celebrates your joy without envy, who holds your sorrow without turning away, something miraculous takes root in your nervous system.

I have lived this lesson across many borders. In Malaysia, my childhood was shaped by the gentle loyalty of school friends who knew my laughter and longing before either had a name. And Cikgu Fauziah, my teacher at boarding school, who recognised that my wild energy was not a flaw to be managed but a spark to be cherished. Her belief offered a rare kind of safety — the sense that even in my untamed moments, I was worthy of encouragement, not correction. In Malay, we call this *silaturrahim**: the sacred thread of kinship and friendship, woven through loyalty, mercy, and trust.

When I moved to England, the pattern continued. New friends like Salayha and Isobel became anchors, each meeting me at a different threshold of becoming, each attuning to parts of me still learning the language of courage and belonging. Later, as I stepped into the world of work across more than forty countries, I met mentors and colleagues who saw potential in me long before I could claim it myself. Their faith — sometimes delivered as challenge, sometimes as kindness — became part of the scaffolding on which I built my life.

This is not luck. It is the deep truth that humans are wired for connection. Even before language, an infant's first communication is not words but touch, gaze, and the warmth of another's arms. That need never leaves us. It travels with us across every border, every time zone.

When you laugh with a friend, when you cry together, when you risk showing the wild, unedited truth of who you are, your body responds as if you are home. Stress softens. Muscles unclench. The heartbeat steadies. This is the biology of trust.

Polyvagal† theory adds to this picture: when we feel safe with another, the body shifts from defence to openness. The nervous system relaxes its guard. We rest, relate, grow — together.

And when connection is real, your whole system knows.

* *Silaturrahim*: the sacred thread of kinship and friendship, rooted in loyalty, mercy, and trust.

† *Polyvagal theory*: safety in connection shifts the body from defence to openness.

Mirror neurons light up in synchrony, joy multiplies when shared, grief ripples tenderly across a family, laughter spreads like flame through a room. Even across years and oceans, a single message from Wa, Julie, or Yana can lift me out of darkness with a memory, a joke, or a Hari Raya song.

Cultures across the world have always carried this knowing. In Africa, the philosophy of *Ubuntu* says: *I am because we are.* In Malay, we say: *berat sama dipikul, ringan sama dijinjing* — together we carry both heavy and light loads. Belonging is not ornament, but survival.

Modern life sometimes tempts us with digital substitutes — likes, comments, fleeting exchanges on screens. But they cannot compare to the deep safety of being truly known. Technology can extend our reach, yes, but what the nervous system longs for is presence. It knows the difference between novelty and nourishment, between dopamine's spike and oxytocin's steadying calm*. One excites. The other restores.

And so, in this architecture of belonging, true friends become the beams and scaffolding. Their belief builds new courage in us. Their delight gives us permission to imagine a bigger, braver self. With every honest exchange, our sense of isolation shrinks, our nervous system learns to rest, and our spirits stretch into wider, brighter rooms.

To be seen.

To belong.

To matter.

This is not only the language of the soul — it is the oldest language of the body.

It is the way we survive.

It is the way we become.

* *Dopamine vs. Oxytocin:* novelty excites, but only belonging restores.

To Show Up is to Be Found

"As you start to walk on the way, the way appears." — Rumi

Some years ago, I was invited to speak about life as a migrant — about the restless courage of building companies abroad as a Malaysian woman far from home. At the end of one interview, after I had shared stories of airports and failures, of reinvention and resilience, the interviewer leaned in and asked quietly:

What would you tell others standing where you once stood?

For a moment I felt the weight of it — the ache of all the years I had stumbled forward without a map. The question hung in the air, larger than any strategy or plan. And then the answer rose in me with such clarity it surprised even me.

Show up.

Not as slogan. Not as performance. But as the only truth I know: that everything I have built, every door that opened, every friendship that endured, began because I crossed a threshold I was afraid to cross.

It is the mantra that has carried me onto stages, through boardrooms and hospital rooms, through love and loss, through the quiet mornings when doubt pressed heavy on my chest. Again and again, showing up — messy, unprepared, imperfect — has been the bridge from fear to possibility.

If there is one piece of advice I would give to anyone longing for more — more belonging, more courage, more meaning — it is this: *show up.*

Again and again, I have seen people falter not for lack of brilliance, but for lack of presence. The greatest doors open for those willing to cross the threshold, trembling but present.

Showing up is the oldest act of faith. Both an offering and a declaration: *Here I am. I will not let fear or self-doubt write my story for me.*

Of course, daring to show up as you are is not easy. It is the oldest risk in the book — to bring your unguarded self into the open and trust that someone will respond not with judgment but with recognition. Yet both science and soul remind us: you cannot find your people while pretending to be someone else. Resonance only arrives when you bring your true frequency to the table — your voice, your quirks, your hopes, your heartbreaks.

And showing up is not one grand leap. It is a daily practice. To show up once is a spark; to show up again and again is how the fire is built. Sometimes it is as simple as answering an invitation, returning a call, or letting your voice tremble in a room full of certainty. Often, it is the quietest, bravest act of the day.

My entire adult life has been lived in-between: not quite traditional enough for some, not quite Western enough for others. Too modern for the Muslim, too foreign for the French. Always crossing borders both visible and invisible. This in-betweenness is simply who I am — not something to glorify, not something to regret.

Yes, sometimes it hurts. The ache of not belonging fully here or there is real. But I have learned, often painfully, that it hurts far more to carve away pieces of myself just to fit. At times, being who I am has unsettled those who prefer easy categories. A Muslim, but not veiled. A woman married to a white man. A mother raising children who do not speak much Malay. These are my truths. They have drawn judgment from those who see identity as a checklist rather than a living, evolving story.

And yet, I have found peace in not fitting neatly anywhere. The pain of not belonging softens, and I begin to love the mosaic of who I am. When I show up in my wholeness, I draw others who love me for all of it — not despite, but because of it.

Showing up as I am — rooted and restless, whole and contradictory — has not left me lonely. It has led me to my true people: not those who measure or manage my belonging, but those who cherish it. Those who see the fullness of my mosaic and welcome it.

Authenticity, I have learned, is not about being special or

different, but about being real. It is the gentle act of self-acceptance: *This is me, and this is enough.*

When you dare to show up in your humanness — messy, brilliant, uncertain, afraid — you send a signal out into the world. And your true people, scattered across continents and seasons, can only find you if you stop hiding.

Consistency matters. To show up again and again is to cast anchor into the changing tides of life. It builds trust in yourself and with others, not as a single act but as a steady drumbeat.

Across centuries and cultures, every person who has changed their life — or the world — began this way: showing up. First awkwardly, then bravely, then with a grace that changes others too.

And when you do? Your body relaxes. Your heart finds its rhythm. You begin to gather a circle — not of convenience, but of chosen kinship. Not just fellow travellers, but fellow builders of the home within.

Let yourself be seen, and you will find yourself mirrored — not only in the eyes of others, but in the quiet confidence of your own soul.

This is how belonging by design begins: with the courage to show up as you are, so that the friends, opportunities, and meanings meant for you can recognise themselves in your light.

What if you showed up, just once, for the thing that scares you or excites you? The way, as Rumi promised, will appear.

Your only task is to arrive as you are.

The rest will meet you on your way.

Lessons from Frida

There is a particular alchemy in the way pain sharpens our senses to what is real, and in the way certain people — like Frida Kahlo* — show us how to turn wounds into works of art and belonging.

---

* *Frida Kahlo (1907–1954)*: More than an artist, she turned her body into canvas

Frida, my personal icon, lived out loud. Her canvases were not just windows into her soul but invitations: *this is what it means to be both scarred and vivid, broken and fiercely alive.* Her life was marked by pain — physical, emotional, existential. Yet she refused to let it make her smaller.

She painted it into colour, into symbol, into testimony. "I am my own muse," she said, and yet her work pulses with others: friends, lovers, kindred spirits, and the heartbreaks that come with loving deeply and living bravely.

She teaches us that real friendships are not about ease or perfection. She surrounded herself with the unruly and the unconventional — the ones who could witness her without flinching, who could hold both her suffering and her joy.

Resonance is not only about pain, but about depth — the kind that comes from having tasted both storm and sunlight.

We are drawn to those who carry laughter lines and grief in equal measure. Leonard Cohen's songs carry longing like prayer. Kendrick Lamar turns struggle into rhythm and resistance into poetry. Their resonance*, like Frida's, is born not from polish but from having walked through fire and still finding music.

Frida's circle was not chosen for comfort, but for courage and truth. She lived the old Spanish wisdom: *"Dime con quién andas y te diré quién eres" — Tell me who you walk with, and I will tell you who you are.* In Malay, too, we say: *"Teman ketawa ramai, teman menangis sukar dicari" — Many will laugh with you, but friends who will cry with you are rare.*

Pain reveals the rare souls who will stay. When we choose friends not for convenience but for their willingness to meet us in

---

and her pain into colour. Her life reminds us that creativity is not escape but transfiguration — sorrow becoming symbol, wound becoming witness.

* *Leonard Cohen & Kendrick Lamar:* Different generations, different geographies, yet both reveal the same truth: when words are steeped in pain and longing, they become prayer. Some voices belong to no single time; they carry the timeless cadence of survival.

both our colours and our shadows, we create a sanctuary — a circle that echoes with truth across time, continents, and cultures.

Science gives language to what Frida embodied. Psychologist Carl Rogers called it *unconditional positive regard** — the gift of being fully seen and accepted. Neuroscientists have shown that empathy lights up our brains as if mirroring another's state, and that compassion can be cultivated through practice†. Research on post-traumatic growth ‡ reminds us that after hardship, our capacity for resonance often deepens: having walked through pain ourselves, we are more able to recognise and honour it in others.

And here lies the paradox. I never knew Frida, yet I find myself in her story. We are separated by oceans, by language, by decades, but in her longing and resilience I recognise something that lives in me too. That, perhaps, is the secret of resonance: we do not have to be the same to find ourselves reflected in another.

The magic of kinship is not sameness, but recognition — the moment we see our hidden aches mirrored in someone else's courage.

As someone whose childhood was marked by turbulence and uprooting, I found in Frida not only an idol but a companion in survival. Like her, I turned to crafts and drawing as alchemy for loneliness and longing — a way to turn sorrow into beauty, and to find belonging through creation.

Frida reminds us: pain is not the opposite of power. It is its source. We cannot always rely on others to name our worth; sometimes we must be our own mirror, our own muse.

---

* *Unconditional Positive Regard:* Carl Rogers offered this phrase, but Frida lived it — and perhaps taught it to herself first. The rarest friendships echo this: *I see your fracture, and I do not look away.*

† *Empathy & Compassion:* Neuroscience shows that our brains mirror each other's joy and sorrow. But beyond the scans, what matters is this: when we allow another's ache to enter us, it does not drown us; it expands us.

‡ *Post-Traumatic Growth:* Pain leaves scars, yes — but also openings. After hardship, some discover a greater capacity for tenderness. The fire does not only burn; it forges.

Leonard Cohen once wrote, *"There is a crack in everything, that's how the light gets in."*

Kendrick Lamar raps of survival with a pulse that feels like prayer.

And Frida painted her wounds until they became windows.

Each, in their own way, shows us the same truth: that the fracture is not the end of belonging, but the doorway to it.

Beloved reader, wherever you stand: can you dare, like them, to see yourself whole and vivid — and to claim your life as your canvas?

A Garden of 150

Belonging is never built alone. If the architecture of adulthood asks us to design our own scaffolding, the architecture of community reminds us that our structures are only as strong as the circles we create together.

Across cultures, humanity has always known this. The Malays call it *gotong-royong** — neighbours coming together to build houses, prepare feasts, carry burdens. In Africa, *Ubuntu*† teaches: *I am because we are.*

In the Middle East, hospitality is sacred law: a traveller is offered water, bread, and shelter before a single question is asked. These are not ornaments of culture. They are blueprints of survival. Without them, no one endures.

Anthropologists say our hearts are wired for circles but not circles too large. Robin Dunbar‡ once suggested we can hold about 150 meaningful bonds before the ties begin to fray. Which means

* *Gotong-royong:* In Malay life, neighbours gather not just to help but to weave belonging itself — showing that community is built as much in kitchens and fields as in temples or halls.

† *Ubuntu:* An African wisdom that says *I am because we are* — a reminder that identity is not a possession but a relationship.

‡ *Dunbar's 150*: Our brains can hold only so many true bonds. The number may be science, but the lesson is simple: intimacy is finite, and therefore precious.

every society — no matter how modern — rests not on skyscrapers but on small rings of kinship, trust, and shared responsibility.

Yet modern life tempts us otherwise. We are told to build endlessly, to measure worth by numbers of followers, by the stretch of our networks. But networks are not always communities. A network may open doors or share information, but it will not sit with you in the dark. Community is different. It is not built on numbers but on resonance — the few who will carry weight with you when the lights go dim, who remain when the crowd moves on.

Wisdom traditions have always known this. Rumi called the heart a guesthouse — each feeling, each friend, a visitor to be welcomed, even if only for a season. Hafiz warned: *The small man builds cages for everyone he knows, while the sage builds great spaces.* The Greeks built the agora, a square where voices gathered in questioning and choice. Emily Dickinson wrote softly: *The soul should always stand ajar, ready to welcome the ecstatic experience.*

In my own life, I have blended these. Malaysian hospitality without obligation. Western openness without self-abandonment. I once thought boundaries were walls. Now I see them as the architecture of true welcome. Only when I know the shape of my own heart can I offer it generously, without resentment*.

But modern life complicates this ancient dance. We live with a thousand digital doors, endless notifications, infinite ways to connect. Hospitality now sometimes means replying slowly, or not at all. Accessibility is not the same as availability. You can be everywhere and nowhere at once.

Nature has been my constant teacher. The elephant leads her herd with fierce memory and care, opening the circle only to those who mean no harm. Tigers raise their cubs in hidden sanctuaries,

---

* *Boundaries as hospitality:* To tend the edges of your heart is not to close the door but to make your welcome real — generosity that does not collapse into exhaustion.

teaching that strength includes tenderness. Emperor penguins huddle in the dark, taking turns at the coldest edge. Wolves run in packs, loyal but selective.

Even flowers discern: the acacia offers its blooms only to chosen pollinators, the lotus rises each morning for the sun, the wisteria entwines what can support it, the rose guards its softest beauty with thorns.

Not every seed is meant to take root in your garden. The river does not give its waters to every thirsty reed. Some are meant for the journey, some for the banks. Ask yourself: who brings you rain, and who only stirs dust? Who feels like sunlight after a long winter? Who, like geese in formation, lifts you higher just by flying beside you?

I am often reminded of an old African proverb, written in neon lights in Mardi and Ali's living room in Canary Wharf: *If you want to go fast, go alone. If you want to go far, go together.*

In tending our inner landscape, with both openness and discernment, we create a place where what matters most can thrive. Boundaries are not barriers but the tending of soil, so that what is precious can grow. To choose with care is not selfishness, but wisdom. And like any living garden, boundaries shift with the seasons — expanding, retreating, blossoming as we do. It is the life-long art of becoming both gatekeeper and gardener of the inner world.

And sometimes, in the most unexpected season, a new soul friend appears, like Nona in Amsterdam. Or an old acquaintance returns as kin, like Juliana in Nantes. Both remind me that discernment not only protects what is precious — it creates space for surprise and joy to bloom.

May your garden be tended with both generosity and care, so that what is rare and precious in you has room to blossom.

Nothing is ours, except time.

"What is meant for you will reach you, even if it is beneath two mountains." — Arabic proverb

Some friendships dissolve not in anger, but in frequency. They drift gently between city blocks, time zones, or the tides of busy seasons. Others return years later as if no time had passed — slipping into your WhatsApp, lighting up your phone, reappearing at just the right moment to remind you that even in a world of parallel lives, our stories sometimes overlap again.

A rare few endure migrations, marriages, and reinventions. They know your childhood slang, your family's ghosts, your heartbreaks and triumphs across continents. They hold your stories with reverence, even as you both outgrow the scripts you were handed.

As a girl in Malaysia, I swapped letters with my early crushes, scribbled birthday cards across time zones, and snuck out with Hazeline to dance in Kuala Lumpur clubs on Saturday nights — our make-up too heavy, our confidence too loud. Later, when I left to study abroad, the letters stopped, but the memories stitched themselves quietly into who we became.

In England, staying in touch with my parents meant queuing at the payphone, praying the reverse-charge call would go through — every minute costly, every word precious. Over the years, static-filled lines gave way to emails, then memes and voice notes, then flights that shrank oceans*. The world grew closer, but closeness itself still carried its own geography.

In Amsterdam, I once belonged to a bustling circle of women, neighbours close enough to knock on each other's doors. But when Isabel was diagnosed with her rare condition, my world shrank to

* *Digital kinship*: Migrant and diasporic communities have long sustained bonds through letters, tapes, now voice notes and memes. The medium changes, but the thread — the longing to remain tethered — endures.

hospital corridors and solitary walks. Invitations slowed. Some stopped altogether. One neighbour even unfollowed me online because I forgot to answer her WhatsApp message. The sting of that surprised me. Sometimes those closest in geography become farthest in spirit, while old friends across continents remain your anchors, holding your pain and hope from afar.

Covid redrew the map of connection. Many friendships faded. Yet some group chats became lifelines, old classmates re-emerged, and Zoom quizzes between friends and families became bridges across empty streets and airports.

I learned that what endured was not frequency but depth — the quality of trust, history, and resonance. The circle shifts, and so do we. Some who once felt like home now feel like rooms in a house we have left behind. This is not betrayal, but the rite of passage every soul must make. Some friendships are chapters — finished but never wasted. Others are perennials*, blooming again and again when the season is right.

Letting go can be an act of grace.

There is courage in blessing a friendship for what it was, and tenderness in welcoming back those who return changed — perhaps as a DM, a voice note, or a smile across a café table. The seasons teach us to celebrate the rare friends who grow with us, to grieve the ones who drift away, and to trust the constellations that guide us forward.

Each friendship, whether brief or enduring, leaves an imprint: a lesson, a light, a language only the two of you share. Honour them all — the constants, the constellations, the chapters, the dimmed city lights that shaped you. In this shifting, luminous world, you are never truly alone.

As Seneca† wrote, *"Nothing is ours, except time."*

---

* *Perennials:* In gardening, perennials die back in winter yet return with quiet certainty. So too with friendships that lie dormant for years, only to bloom again when the season is right.

† Seneca reminds us nothing belongs to us but time. Friendship is how we choose

Friendships, too, are gifts of time: some lasting, some fleeting, all transformative. There will be seasons when you are the one who drifts, and seasons when you are the anchor. Both are part of the dance in your home within.

Pause for a moment. Who are the friends who remain in your constellation*, even as the city lights shift? Send them a gentle thought, or a message if you are moved. Gratitude, after all, is its own kind of homecoming.

A Star Wrapped in Skin

Belonging is not a fixed structure but a constellation of stars, shifting and re-forming as we move through the seasons of life. Some stars remain steady, others flare for a moment, and a rare few glow beside us as we change. But belonging is not only about who stands near — it is also about how we learn to see and be seen in the world.

Our nervous systems calm not only with shelter, but with recognition. When someone meets your gaze, remembers your laugh, or listens to the story behind your silence, your body learns: *I am safe. I belong.* Psychologist Barbara Fredrickson calls these "micro-moments" of belonging — fleeting yet powerful sparks that ease stress and remind us we are woven into the living web of the world.

Rituals weave this fabric too: a letter sent without occasion, a memory revisited, a meal shared in ordinary time. For me, it is a voice note from my brother across time zones, a walk along the canal with Isabel, a basket of tomatoes from Christopher's rooftop garden, a stranger's hand holding the door when mine are full.

---

to spend that gift — lending hours, seasons, sometimes years, into each other's keeping.

* *Constellations*: In many traditions, stars are not just light but stories. To call a friend part of your constellation is to say: even across distance, their story helps you navigate your own night sky.

Small gestures become constellations, bright enough to guide us through the ordinariness of days.

Even absence carries presence. The mind cannot always distinguish between a real embrace and a remembered one. Close your eyes and recall a moment of connection — feel your heart soften. The light remains.

Ancient wisdom and modern science echo the same truth: the universe itself is relationship.

Physicists speak of entanglement, particles once linked remaining connected across vast distances. Malay poets call it *rindu,* the soulful ache that stretches across oceans. The Portuguese call it *saudade,* the bittersweet longing for what may never fully return. Both remind us that love and memory live on, even when apart.

To be the light is to bear witness — to see another not as one among many, but as a singular spark in the night. Alan Watts once wrote: *Through our eyes, the universe is perceiving itself. Through our ears, the universe is listening to its harmonies.* Whether you call it stardust or spirit, the truth is the same: each of us is a star wrapped in skin, part of a greater whole.

As above, so below.

As within, so without.

The belonging we search for in the night sky is mirrored in the rituals of recognition and care. The universe and the human heart are reflections of one another — each longing to be seen, each longing to belong.

And if you feel lonely, remember: somewhere, the light you once sent out — years ago or this morning — may be reaching another heart even now.

The universe is wide, but kindness is never wasted.

Tend your micro-moments.

Honour the brief encounters as much as the steady companions.

Be a stargazer, yes — but also be a candle in the window, a glow on a phone, a quiet word of encouragement.

And when the day is done, look up.

You do not need to shine the brightest.

You only need to shine as you are — and trust that in doing so, you will always find your way home within.

Chapter 11

Multiple Belongings

"This place is magical!" — Mei, *My Neighbour Totoro*

Totoro and the Art of Multiplicity

I've never been able to answer the question, 'Where are you really from?' with the crisp assurance the world seems to prefer.

My belonging has always been plural — a mosaic of places, languages, rituals, and memories trailing behind me like a bright string of lanterns in the dusk. I have lived at many tables, in many cities: Kuala Lumpur's humid evenings, the lively pulse of London, the grim skies of Amsterdam, even the sleepy streets of Gütersloh. Each place is a room in the unfolding house of my memory. And sometimes I sense that if life carried me to New York, the olive groves of Puglia, or the lush hills of Chiang Mai, I could learn to belong there too.

The world, for me, is a forest: vast, mysterious, always opening onto new clearings, each with its own invitation to dwell and become. Belonging is not something we inherit, but something we practice — like hospitality, like generosity, like wonder.

Perhaps this is why, when I search for a metaphor for how I

move through the world, I turn to Totoro*, the whimsical forest spirit from *My Neighbour Totoro.* Totoro is a gentle giant with an open heart, who makes a home of the whole forest and welcomes lost children and wandering souls alike. I love his way of being: quietly magical, never demanding anyone shrink themselves to belong.

I do not pretend to be as gentle or mythic as Totoro, but I am inspired by his spirit: to embody multiplicity with generosity. To welcome contradictions. To live with a sense of enchantment, seeing each new place as part of one great forest of becoming.

Japan deepened this truth in me. As a child of 1980s Malaysia, I grew up during the *Look East*† campaign, when our government encouraged us to draw inspiration from Japanese values: discipline, humility, and the dignity of ritual. Japan became, for me, more than a faraway country. It became an idea — a way of seeing.

When a Japanese choir visited my primary school on Jalan Gurney, I befriended Mitsumi Takeda. I don't remember her face clearly, but I remember my first thought: she looked like a doll. We became pen pals, sending letters between Kuala Lumpur and Nagasaki. Mitsumi tucked origami dolls into her envelopes, folded from delicate *washi,*‡ arriving like small treasures for a hopeful Malay girl. I displayed them on my bookshelf, a private museum of belonging across distance. Even now, when I seek peace, I think of those dolls — fragile, precise, carrying a whole philosophy of care.

Zen gave me language for what I had already intuited. Home is not a building but a presence: a breath, a moment, a single unhurried cup of tea. The Japanese speak of *uchi* (inside) and *soto*

---

* *Totoro:* A forest spirit from Studio Ghibli's 1988 film, Totoro became a global icon of gentle belonging — a reminder that home can be the whole forest, open to all who wander.

† *Look East:* Malaysia's 1980s campaign urging citizens to learn from Japanese discipline and humility — proof that cultural values can be shared across borders.

‡ *Washi:* Traditional Japanese handmade paper, delicate yet resilient.

(outside), of thresholds between inner and outer worlds. A house becomes a home through ritual: the sweeping of a doorstep, the sharing of rice, the placing of a single ikebana stem. Zen gardens teach us *wabi-sabi* [*]— the beauty of imperfection and impermanence — reminding us that emptiness is not absence but space for everything else to breathe.

This is why Japanese notions of home resonate with my Malay heart. Both cultures know that home is more than shelter: it is memory, ritual, patience, and becoming.

Sometimes home is as simple as bottles of spice in a kitchen, my laptop on a table, my daughters' laughter echoing down a hallway, or David's voice calling Isabel away from the fridge in another room. They are the steady centre of my wandering compass.

I have learned that belonging can fit into a single suitcase or spill across the canals of de Jordaan. It can travel on aeroplanes, flicker across WhatsApp, or live in voices carried across time zones. My family and friends travel with me, not only in photographs but in the architecture of my heart.

Neuroscience affirms what Totoro and Japan had already taught me. David Eagleman calls the brain "a team of rivals"[†] — not one fixed self but many voices negotiating who we are. Psychology speaks of multipotentiality[‡] — the ability to hold many gifts, many identities, at once. To be plural is not confusion. It is capacity.

Like Totoro, I too can be contradictory and still whole. My home within is the hand that holds the strings of a many-coloured kite, soaring across continents. Every string is a place, a memory, a friendship, a flavour. None severed. All connected.

---

* *Wabi-Sabi:* The Japanese art of seeing beauty in imperfection and impermanence — a truth mirrored in migration and memory.

† *Team of Rivals:* Eagleman's phrase for the brain's many voices — teaching us that contradiction is part of being human.

‡ *Multipotentiality:* The gift of holding many lives within one life — not scattered, but whole.

Kokoro no furusato. The heart's true home.

Ichi-go ichi-e. One time, one meeting.

Every place, every friendship, every moment of belonging is unrepeatable, precious, part of the shimmering magic of being alive.

And when I am uncertain, I return to this: home is not always where you began, but where you allow life's imperfections and fleeting moments to be enough — trusting the wisdom of *wabi-sabi,* that beauty is found in the simple, the weathered, and the ever-changing.

The Kitchen Has No Border

If you ask me about home, I will not point to a single place on a map. I will invite you to the table in my kitchen.

In Asia, to ask after someone's heart, you ask after their hunger. Among Malaysians — whether Malay, Chinese, Indian, Iban, or Baba-Nyonya — food is the universal greeting. We say *"Dah makan?"* ("Have you eaten?")*, not *"How are you?"* It is our way of asking if you are well, if you are loved, if you are part of us.

Across the Malay archipelago, the table is the most honest map of who we are. Indonesians might offer *nasi goreng* or *rendang* to welcome a stranger. Filipinos gather around *kamayan* feasts, eating with their hands in a circle of kinship. Singaporeans queue for the best laksa or chicken rice, knowing the meal is never just about filling the stomach but about stitching together community. In Thailand, a meal is not complete unless it is shared. In Vietnam, grandmothers roll rice paper at the table while stories unravel. In Cambodia, a simple bowl of *amok* brings the family home after a long day apart.

My own family, scattered but connected by recipes and long-

* *"Dah makan?"* — Across Asia, to ask if someone has eaten is to ask if they are cared for. Hunger and belonging are inseparable.

ing, asks *"Sudah makan?"* as shorthand for *"I care about you. Come home."*

Even our most beloved dishes carry the memory of migration*: *kaya* toast born of *Hainanese* cooks and colonial bread, *roti canai* descended from Indian paratha, seri *kaya* inspired by custards but fragrant with *pandan*, *pandan* chiffon cake — a colonial sponge turned Southeast Asian icon.

Everyone who knows me knows: I am most at home in my kitchen. If you have ever touched my heart, you have been fed at my table — whether with an elaborate feast or simply a warm slice of sourdough. Feeding others has always been my quiet love language. To gather people — no matter their passport or the God they worship — around my table is how I fill my own bowl.

Because we all know: you cannot pour from an empty bowl. Every ladle of soup, every shared story, is as much for me as for you. It is my way of saying: *you belong here.*

Food, for me, is not just sustenance. It is celebration, solace, survival. It is what unites the village, the festival, the mourning house, the reunion dinner. The table is where strangers become kin, where generations pass wisdom by the ladle, where journeys end — no matter how far we have wandered.

Perhaps that is why, even now, every border I cross, I begin with food. To taste is to belong, if only for a moment. To sit at someone's table is to accept their story and to offer your own. A meal can do what maps and treaties never can: turn suspicion into laughter, loss into memory, and longing into home.

In Amsterdam, home is homemade *sambal* in my fridge, its spice as potent as any memory of Kuala Lumpur *mamak* stalls†. It is rolling pastry for a French *galette*, stirring *laksa* broth rich with lemongrass, and watching my daughters slather peanut butter on

* *Hybrid dishes:* Kaya toast, roti canai, pandan chiffon — recipes are migrations in edible form, proof that cultures mingle most easily at the table.

† *Mamak stalls:* Malaysia's 24-hour open-air kitchens, where every race and faith meet over roti canai and teh tarik — food as democracy.

baguette — delighted, unconfused. A single meal might carry five histories: the spice of my ancestors, the bread of my migrations, the sweetness of unexpected friendships. Some days, I am rice and *rendang*. Other days, sourdough and French *comté*. Some afternoons I am Dutch cream puffs and tea, while *sambal tumis belacan* fills the air with ache and possibility.

My home is not a single recipe. It is a feast, a gathering where nothing is left out and every guest brings their own story to the pot.

Human history itself is written in kitchens. Archaeologists have found traces of communal meals* in caves 12,000 years old. The world's oldest bread was baked 14,000 years ago on Jordanian stones; China's earliest noodles stretch back millennia. Banquets have marked every great milestone — weddings, treaties, harvests, peace. To break bread has always been to turn strangers into guests. Even now, diplomacy is sealed not only by ink, but by shared meals.

In my own kitchen, I hope to create this quiet alchemy: a space where bread and laughter dissolve resentments, where stories pass hands more easily than judgments, where feeding becomes peace. I have seen misunderstandings melt over chicken rice, friendships begin with the passing of salt.

Taste itself is memory. The gustatory cortex is braided with the amygdala and hippocampus, where emotion and memory live. A spoonful of laksa can carry you back decades. The scent of *pandan* in a Dutch *toko*† can ache like a homecoming. French salted butter can transport me to a country not yet lived in but waiting. Scientists call this the Proustian‡ effect: when flavour or scent unlocks not only an image but the texture of belonging itself.

* *Commensality*: Anthropologists call it the practice of eating together. To share a meal is to say: *you are no longer stranger, but guest.*

† *Tokos in the Netherlands*: Migrant food shops that bridge colonial histories and modern cravings, carrying sambal and pandan into Dutch streets.

‡ *Proustian memory:* Taste and scent unlock memory faster than sight or sound — the kitchen as time machine.

Flavour is an alchemist.

Tamarind, cinnamon, olives — they open hidden doors in the mind, summoning people and places we thought we had forgotten.

To taste is to remember. And when we share food, we share not only recipes but centuries of migration, celebration, and survival.

Every cuisine is a living archive of geography, climate, faith, and trade.

To eat another's food is to borrow their ancestors for a meal, to learn how their rivers and histories have mingled. Flavour becomes a quiet diplomacy: proof that what is foreign can become beloved, that what is strange can become sustenance.

Food is not only nourishment. It is a rehearsal for empathy. When we eat together, we practice taking in what is different, making it part of us, and being changed by it.

I truly believe, if every nation could sit at one another's tables, we would see the world differently. We might recognise our own longings in another's stew, our grandmother's love in someone else's festival dish. Flavour is a universal language, one that predates borders and outlasts them.

To share a table is to build a bridge.

Not to erase difference, but to taste its beauty.

The feast is always more delicious, and the world more possible, when no one is left hungry and every story is welcome in the pot.

Everyone is welcome to bring their flavour to my table, as I share mine. Because to share is how I live, and this, too, is my home. After all, as the Germans say, *Liebe geht durch den Magen* — love finds its way through the stomach.

In the kitchen, there are no borders.

Only the grace of welcome, and the promise of return.

Nina Aziz Justin

An Invitation to My "Peace Party"

"O mankind! We created you from a single pair of a male and a female, and made you into nations and tribes so that you may know one another... Verily, the most honoured of you in the sight of Allah is the most righteous among you."
— Qur'an 49:13

I am Malaysian in my bones. I feel it in the way I *salam*[*] with both hands resting on my heart and the gentle bow of my head, in the way I reach for coconut milk instead of cream, in the way I say *makan dulu* — eat first, it is love.

But I am also, irrevocably, a citizen of the world.

My friendships are a constellation: Jewish friends who light Shabbat candles on Friday nights, Christian friends who have prayed for my children, atheist friends who hold my questions with kindness. I am welcomed at Ramadan iftars, at Diwali and Christmas, at Eid and Easter, and each time I am reminded: allegiance can be layered; loyalty can be wide.

And yet I know the invisible lines that shaped our divisions. Labels like "First World" and "Third World" were never about geography, but power[†]. They hardened into habit — a way of ranking, forgetting that those once pushed aside were heirs to ancient civilisations of science, poetry, and art.

History left us scars of "divide and rule." Sometimes those scars reopened into weapons. The wound between Muslims and Jews deepens with each tragedy in Palestine and Gaza, layered with the West's grief of the Holocaust. At times I feel both stories in my chest — each aching to be understood, each afraid to be forgotten.

---

[*] *Salam:* The Malay greeting — gentle handshake, hand to the heart — a gesture that says, "This comes from me sincerely."

[†] *Inherited Divisions:* Phrases like "First/Third World" were political shorthand from the Cold War that became habit, shaping how nations saw each other.

But my life refuses that script. My Jewish friends — Alorani, Liron, Alain — are as dear to me as any Muslim sister or brother. They have welcomed me, laughed with me, prayed for my children, held me in grief. In their friendship, I find proof that kindness can outlast rivalry. There is nothing holy in hating another simply because history and politics told us to.

Being a bridge can mean being battered by two storms, loving people on both sides who cannot yet recognise each other's pain. In those moments I whisper *dua* — the prayer of the heart in Islam, sometimes spoken, sometimes silent, always a reaching — that the wounds will soften, that grief will be shared, that trust will be rebuilt.

I have seen hope not only at dinner tables, but in boardrooms and airports, in co-working spaces and midnight calls. Across continents, kindness and cruelty wear every accent. Humanity's spectrum is not East or West, Muslim or Jew — it is simply human, capable of both beauty and harm.

The answer, I know, begins inside: in the home within.

That is where the first border falls, the first invitation is made.

To live with a home within is to insist that every human is worthy — of dignity, kinship, a chance to belong. Mandela said it best: no one is born hating; if we can learn to hate, we can learn to love.

Some days I am weary of being a bridge. Most days I know it is sacred work. For though the ache of belonging everywhere and nowhere is real, so too is the miracle of finding again and again that kindness is possible: tables where laughter dissolves suspicion, where second helpings are offered without hesitation, where stories of who we are and who we could be are told anew.

This is the inheritance I want for my children: not a single narrative, but many. In our home we mark Chinese New Year, Aidilfitri, Aidiladha, Diwali, Rosh Hashanah, Christmas, and

Easter*. Camilla once joked we should even add Afghanistan's national day, just to celebrate it.

We celebrate humanity. We celebrate life. Not as doctrine, but as rituals of kinship and joy.

I have never felt distance between races unless unkindness built it. My only aversion is to cruelty disguised as tradition, fear masquerading as purity. I belong where there is generosity, laughter, and an open seat at the table.

To me, the world is not a closed system of rivalry. It is a long table, a meeting room, a late-night message thread woven with invisible wires linking hearts across continents. Sometimes connection is as simple as "*Motek*!† It is a *balagan*‡ here!" in the dark, a note from Liron in Tel Aviv — proof that love can leap over lines history tried to carve in stone.

Connection is not privilege. It is birthright.

It asks only that we meet eye to eye, heart to heart, across whatever distances remain.

We are all longing to belong.

Perhaps that is what binds us most: the stubborn hope that even across old wounds, we will still reach for the other hand — for a *salam*, for a *shalom*.

No wound, no difference, no story is worth the taking of a single life.

May our hands meet in peace, not in harm.

May the bridges we build never be paved with blood, but with the simple, stubborn acts of listening and love. My path has wandered between cultures, questions, and teachers.

---

* *Festivals*: Iftar, Aidilfitri, Aidiladha, Chinese New Year, Diwali, Rosh Hashanah, Christmas, Easter — each one a different lantern, yet all light the same truth: joy multiplies when shared.

† *Motek* (מותק): A Hebrew term of endearment, like "sweetheart" or "darling." Often tossed lightly into everyday messages, it carries warmth — a reminder that affection can travel across borders in a single word.

‡ *Balagan* (בלגן): A Hebrew word meaning "mess" or "chaos," used with humour and affection. It acknowledges life's disorder without judgment — the way families, friendships, or even histories can be tangled, yet still full of love.

I do not write as someone with all the answers, but as someone who keeps searching — imperfect, persistent — in the name of peace.

My *dua*[*], whispered silent and aloud:

May we become, in our own ways, a home within the world for each other. Never builders of harm. Always builders of peace.

And may we remember: peace is not abstract.

It is a promise we renew in the daily work of love.

We Are Nature

Nature teaches this truth again and again: nothing alive is made of just one thing.

Sand, whether beneath my feet on the shores of Melaka where I took my first steps or those clinging to the spaces between Isabel's toes on Wijk aan Zee, is a testament to multiplicity. Each grain began as mountain or coral or shell — shaped by time, broken by wind and water, carried across continents. In a single fistful of sand, you hold the memory of volcanoes, forests, stone, and sea. A shoreline is not a boundary but a gathering, a festival of difference.

Blood, too, tells a many-layered story. In my family, lineages stretch across the Malay archipelago: Bugis sailors, Minangkabau women, Chinese merchants, Tamil weavers, Arab traders, and the echoes of colonial arrivals. I see it in our faces, hear it in our tongues. My mother's *char kway teow* — the wok breathing fire into flat rice noodles with cockles, soy, and *sambal* — is more than a dish. It is Teochew[†] roots and Penang spice routes, strangers becoming kin.

Even our DNA carries crossings. My niece Nia's eyes hold

* *Dua* — a prayer of the heart, spoken or silent, a reaching toward the Divine.

† *Teochew roots:* Migrants from southern China who carried their wok-fired flavours across Southeast Asia, blending spice routes and local ingredients into beloved dishes like *char kway teow*.

traces of Indian heritage from my maternal grandmother's family, once civil servants brought to Malaya[*]. My cousins bear Chinese features, some look Indian, some like me — a bit of everything. Sometimes I glimpse a ring of greyish blue in my eyes, an unexpected inheritance in Southeast Asia. In one family tree, the world gathers.

Science affirms what families already show us: there is no pure lineage.[†] Every body is a tapestry.

Within us live trillions of microbes — collaborators shaping our digestion[‡], immunity, even our moods. Even our own skin is not singular. We are colonies, ecosystems, networks in motion.

The forest whispers the same truth. Trees feed each other through underground fungal webs, sending strength from the elders — Mother Trees [§]— to the saplings. Coral reefs, bees, and penguins remind us that survival is communal. Even the air we breathe is borrowed, molecules shared by mountains, forests, cities, and lungs. Every drop of rain carries memory[#], every breath a history.

Above us, the cosmos repeats the lesson.

The atoms in our bones were born in ancient stars[○]: hydrogen from the dawn of time, iron from supernovae, calcium from ashes of worlds before.

The universe itself is relationship — planets circling suns,

---

* *Indian crossings:* Families brought by the British to Malaya as teachers, clerks, labourers — leaving behind languages, foods, and faith woven into Malaysia's fabric.

† *Shared ancestry*: Geneticist Svante Pääbo showed that every human carries traces of ancient Neanderthals and Denisovans — proof that "purity" is a myth; we are all crossings.

‡ *The second brain:* Our bodies are home to trillions of microbes that shape mood, immunity, and digestion. Even within our own skin, we are community.

§ *Mother Trees:* In forests, old giants feed the saplings through underground fungal webs — quiet proof that survival depends on generosity, not isolation.

Rain memory: Each drop carries a record of oceans, mountains, and climates across time — to drink is to inherit history.

○ *Star-stuff:* The calcium in our bones, the iron in our blood, the oxygen we breathe — all forged in ancient stars. We carry galaxies within us.

galaxies spiraling among billions. Nowhere is there only one. Everywhere is interplay, exchange, transformation.

Our human world is no different. Despite passports and borders, life is already plural. English itself is stitched from many tongues. America is a patchwork of migrations and reinventions. Singapore, Britain, Australia — each hums with the mingling of kitchens, prayers, and languages.

Wisdom traditions have always known this: Heraclitus said, "Nothing endures but change." The I Ching reminds us that all under heaven moves and transforms. Rumi whispers, "You are not a drop in the ocean. You are the entire ocean in a drop."

Multiplicity is not a flaw but a form of magic — permission to be many, to belong in more than one world, to taste life in many flavours. Psychologists call some of us multipotentialites* — souls who thrive across fields, weaving art with science, faith with philosophy.

Neuroscience† shows that stretching ourselves in this way makes the brain more creative, more resilient. Novelty multiplies us. Ambiguity strengthens us.

So it is not strange to feel a sense of many belongings. If anything, it is our most natural state.

To be human is to be multilayered — history braided with possibility, ancestry blended with imagination, belonging stitched from memory and hope.

Multiplicity is not a problem to solve. It is the inheritance of sand, blood, and stardust.

The world was never designed for purity. It was shaped for mingling, meeting, and change — as long as the sun rises over oceans and mountains.

This is not my wisdom alone. It is the patient lesson of sand

---

* *Multipotentialite*: A soul who thrives in many callings at once, weaving seemingly separate gifts into one mosaic of becoming.

† *Plastic brains:* Neuroscience shows that novelty and variety strengthen our neural pathways — proving that curiosity itself is a form of resilience.

and blood, of water and wind, of every crossing that came before and every crossing still to come.

The world is wide and woven, and so are you.

May your home within be spacious enough to hold all your crossings, and tender enough to belong everywhere.

Chapter 12

The Sacred Intuition

Wan Jah's Dream

I am carried back to the days and nights before I left Malaysia for the UK, the air in my mother's house heavy with a kind of knowing no map could show.

My paternal grandmother, Wan Jah, was capable of *menilik nasib** — fortune-telling without books or schooling, reading dreams and omens in nature as others read letters on a page. She trusted the birds, the butterflies, the weather, the whispers between worlds.

On the eve of my departure, Wan Jah telephoned my mother, her former daughter-in-law, with a warning in the language of symbols. She had dreamt of the mango tree in front of my mother's house, its branches heavy with golden fruit. Strangers came and plucked them, one by one.

"If she goes across the ocean," she said, her voice trembling. "She will never live here again."

My mother relayed the message, her modern mind dismissing

* *Menilik nasib*: A Malay phrase for "reading fate," often through dreams or natural signs.

it as superstition, yet her face clouded with unease. I, too, wanted to brush it away, but my teenage heart sank with the weight of it. Still, even then, I knew my lessons waited elsewhere. Malaysia felt too small for the ache inside me.

All that turmoil meant I did not take the first flight my father had bought. The delay was filled with family discussions and confusion. But a few nights later, I left anyway, carrying the image of the mango tree and Wan Jah's warning all the way to London Heathrow.

I remember peering through the small window of MH002 as Kuala Lumpur slipped away — the city's lights fading into the black of night, the land dissolving into cloud. Sometimes I wonder if, as I left, I carried the scent of those mangoes with me: sweetness and loss, abundance and letting go, ripe fruit gathered for a journey invisible to others.

Only years later did I begin to understand the deeper currents beneath that dream. Science now has words for what Wan Jah called a warning: intergenerational intuition, ancestral memory, the mysterious tuning of one life to another.

Across cultures, this knowing is honoured. Ancestors appear in dreams, visions pass through bloodlines*, bone memory† stirs before words. The Sufi heart, the Chinese pulse, the Jewish‡ spark — each points to the same mystery: what we call intuition is rarely solitary, but a chorus of voices urging us to listen.

Neuroscience and epigenetics suggest the same — that the griefs and hopes of our ancestors can shape our nervous systems, influencing how we respond to the world before we are even conscious of it.

This is the mystery of limbic resonance: our oldest brain struc-

* *Intergenerational intuition:* Ancestral experiences can leave traces in us — sometimes felt as instinct, sometimes as heaviness, sometimes as guidance.

† *Bone memory*: In many Indigenous traditions, wisdom is said to live in the body itself, surfacing before words.

‡ Sparks of soul (*nitzotzot shel neshama*): In Jewish mysticism, fragments of divine light carried across generations.

tures tuned not only to our own experience but to the songs and silences of generations.

In families where sorrow was unspoken, children may inherit a heaviness they cannot name. In lineages where dreams were trusted, a granddaughter may find herself guided by visions she never dreamt.

Wan Jah needed no textbooks. She trusted her body as an antenna, attuned by the long line of women who survived by feeling what could not be named.

For those who live between worlds, intuition is not luxury but compass — survival kit and soul kit. Maps fail. Customs shift. What is home in one place vanishes in another. In those moments, intuition is the truest guide.

You learn to read the room where your accent is strange, sense when to lean in or step back, trust the prick in your gut or the lift in your heart. And yet, I have often paid the price of ignoring it. Every time I silenced the tug of knowing and chose logic instead, it cost me dearly. Heartache. Disappointment. The hidden despair of being lost in my own story.

I have learned, sometimes painfully, that intuition is rarely loud, rarely convenient — but always faithful. Now I ask not just, *Does this make sense?* but *Does this feel like home?*

Because the true work of building the home within is returning to that childlike way of knowing: open, receptive, brave. Remembering what our bodies never forgot: that we belong to ourselves, that we belong to each other, that we belong to the wisdom flowing in our bones.

And each time I honour that quiet pull, the home within grows a little wider, a little safer, a little truer.

Wan Jah passed while I was in England. Her dream proved true: I never lived in Malaysia again.

Compass, Not Contraband

Long before Western systems swept across continents, most cultures honoured inner knowing as essential, not optional.

The oldest stories told by firesides and beneath open skies were stitched together from dreams, omens, and the wisdom of the body. People everywhere survived by reading the language of intuition: the shiver before a storm, the silence of animals before an earthquake, the heaviness in the chest when someone untrustworthy entered a room.

The Greeks looked to Delphi, the Norse to their dream-songs, the Egyptians to visions of the night. In Australia, songlines* mapped the land; in West Africa, Ifá divination† aligned the soul with destiny. Everywhere, children were taught not only to obey their elders but to listen to their own hearts. Life was too uncertain, nature too powerful, for reason alone to suffice.

But the ground shifted. The Enlightenment enthroned rationality, and what could not be measured was cast aside as superstition. Descartes declared, *"I think, therefore I am,"* and the world split mind from body, fact from feeling.

Schools taught children to silence their instincts in favour of correct answers, workplaces rewarded proof over presence, even when the heart knew otherwise.

Modernity made a god not only of reason, but of control. Yet life, like weather, like love, was never meant to be managed into certainty.

The deeper wisdom has always been to dance with the unknown. Intuition is not the rejection of intelligence, but its forgotten partner — the compass that steadies us when maps run out.

---

* *Songlines:* In Aboriginal tradition, routes across the land carried in song, blending geography, story, and spirit — proof that memory and map can be one.

† *Ifá divination:* A Yoruba system that reads patterns in palm nuts or chains, not as superstition but as dialogue with destiny.

For those who live across cultures, intuition is not a luxury but survival. The rules change, the language shifts, and the body must often guide where the mind cannot.

Neuroscience shows that when the rational brain is overwhelmed by novelty, older systems step forward: the limbic brain and the "gut brain"* scan for danger, interpret micro-signals, and make decisions in real time. Migrants, expatriates, and refugees often speak of gut feelings, hunches, or knowing without knowing how. Their lives demand it.

I learned this most vividly in motherhood. When my daughter Isabel was four months old, I knew she was different. It was in the way she pressed her wrists against her body, the fix in her gaze, the deep silence in her eyes. It was not fear but bone-deep knowing, felt long before it could be named.

At her crèche, the Dutch childminder, with more than twenty years of experience, teased me gently: *"Don't be an Asian tiger mum!"* She smiled as I pressed her with questions — had she noticed anything different in Isabel's movements, her gaze, the way she responded? With her long experience, she reassured me all was well, brushing aside my unease.

Doctors, too, offered comfort. Yet something in me refused to quiet down. I carried my questions to the GGD, the Dutch municipal health service, insisting through layers of protocol and doubt. It took nearly three years of persistence, scans, and genetic testing before the truth emerged: Isabel had Trip12, an extremely rare neurological condition, with only twenty-one known cases in the world in 2017.

The diagnosis brought grief but also relief. I was not imagining things. My intuition had been right all along, even when no one — not the professionals, not even David, my husband — could see what I felt.

---

* *Gut brain:* The enteric nervous system, a vast network of neurons in the digestive tract, communicating directly with the brain and shaping instinctive decision-making.

Science now affirms what mothers have always carried. Pregnancy and attachment prime the maternal brain for deep attunement, sharpening regions linked to empathy and vigilance. This "maternal sixth sense"* is not myth but adaptation, echoed across the animal kingdom.

Yet intuition is not confined to mothers.

Mirror neurons† and emotional resonance allow all of us — fathers, friends, lovers, even strangers — to sense what another feels, if we pay attention.

So why do so many of us stop listening? Because the world trains us to. Rational thought is rewarded; bodily wisdom dismissed.

Neuroscientist Daniel Kahneman explains how our slower, deliberate reasoning often overrides the fast, intuitive knowing that once kept our ancestors alive. To trust your gut in a culture that prizes proof can feel risky, even rebellious.

But the Tao Te Ching counsels: *"At the centre of your being, you have the answer."*

Rumi reminds: *"There is a voice that doesn't use words. Listen."*

And Blaise Pascal confessed: *"The heart has its reasons which reason does not know."*

Intuition is not contraband. It is compass. To live without it is to live half awake. To trust it is to risk being wrong — but also to risk being wholly, beautifully alive.

Intuition is the inheritance of every body that has survived, every heart that has ever listened. It is the compass that has always been there, waiting to guide us home within.

---

* *Maternal sixth sense:* Brain changes in pregnancy and early motherhood heighten empathy and vigilance — not myth, but biology tuned for care.

† *Mirror neurons:* Brain cells that fire when we act or witness another's action, the neural basis of empathy and resonance.

The Gut of Knowledge

Intuition is often dismissed as superstition, as if it belongs only to grandmothers and poets, monks and mystics. Yet every body is born with it: an inbuilt guidance system honed over millennia of survival.

Long before language or maps, humans lived by reading the silent signals of the body — the shiver before a storm, the stillness of animals before an earthquake, the prickle of unease when someone entered the room. This was not fantasy, but biology.

Neuroscience calls it *interoception* — the ability to sense the inner state of our bodies. The gut, sometimes called our "second brain," is lined with more than a hundred million neurons, more than the spinal cord. It listens, remembers, decides. It churns not only food, but feeling — butterflies, dread, longing, relief. That twist in your stomach or warmth in your chest is not random. It is data. It is the body speaking before the mind can catch up.

At nineteen I took the cheapest route home and found myself stranded for five days in Karachi — walking the tarmac at Kalam Azad airport, intimidated by men with rifles. Intuition became my only companion. It steered me away from a man at dinner who, between mouthfuls of *biryani*, offered marriage and promises of Peshawar. It told me not to answer the door when notes slipped beneath it, and it nudged me toward a group of women on the beach when I felt watched. I knew no language, no custom, but my body recognised the patterns — the change in voices, the static charge in the air, the weight of lingering eyes. I survived those days not by calculation, but by listening to the ancient circuitry humming beneath my skin.

Those who cross borders — migrants, nomads, artists, mothers — often sharpen this radar. Each crossing strips away the familiar, demanding that you read the unspoken. When the mind hesitates, the gut leads.

Artists have long trusted this inheritance. Kandinsky spoke of *innere Notwendigkeit** — "inner necessity" — the unseen force that compelled his hand. He wrote: *"Jede Kunstform ist die Tochter ihrer Zeit, und oft die Mutter unserer Gefühle"* — "Every work of art is the child of its age, and often the mother of our emotions." For him, true creation was never imitation but the honest listening to that inner pulse.

Miles Davis played first, naming it later. Georgia O'Keeffe admitted her paintings gave form to things she had no words for.

Intuition is the brushstroke, the note, the gesture that rises before the mind explains it†.

Entrepreneurs, too, honour this knowing. Steve Jobs once said intuition was "more powerful than intellect." Oprah Winfrey has spoken of her biggest decisions narrowing down to a single question: *Does this feel right?* In boardrooms as much as in studios, intuition often makes the difference between spotting opportunity or being left behind.

Wisdom traditions echo the same truth. In Sufi teaching, the heart is said to have an eye of its own. The Māori speak of *wairua*‡ — the spirit sensed before it is seen. Each suggests what we forget too easily: intuition is not contraband. It is our first inheritance.

And yet, in a world obsessed with certainty, we are taught to mistrust it. To second-guess what our body already knows. Neuroscientist Daniel Kahneman showed how slow, deliberate reasoning often overrides the fast, intuitive knowing that once kept our ancestors alive. To trust your gut in a culture that prizes proof can feel risky, even rebellious.

---

* *Innere Notwendigkeit*: Kandinsky's phrase means "inner necessity" — a reminder that true creation begins not with rules, but with listening to the unseen impulse that insists on being expressed.

† *Butterflies in the stomach*: Ancient physicians already saw the gut as a seat of emotion. Modern science confirms the enteric nervous system communicates directly with the brain, giving language to feelings the heart once carried alone.

‡ *Wairua*: In Māori thought, wairua is the spirit that flows through all things. It is felt rather than seen, guiding choices and connecting people with land, ancestors, and one another.

But intuition is not the enemy of reason — it is its forgotten partner. To live without it is to live half awake.

And so I return again and again to that inner compass. To trust it is to risk being wrong, but also to risk being wholly, beautifully alive*. Intuition is the inheritance of every body that has ever survived, every heart that has ever listened. It is the compass that has always been there, waiting to guide us home within.

Symphony

Modern neuroscience and ancient wisdom meet at the same truth: the body is not a collection of parts, but a living symphony.

There are rare moments when the inner orchestra swells and, with every cell, you simply know:

this is right.

The gut, the heart, and the mind move together in quiet synchrony, each attuned, each note ringing true.

Gentle practices — prayer, meditation, heart-focused breathing, or simply pausing to notice your breath — invite this music of coherence†.

The breath steadies.

The heart softens.

The mind clears.

Choices that once felt heavy become lighter, almost effortless.

This is not just poetry. The heart carries its own intelligence — a network of nerves that remembers, learns, and guides. The gut, with its "second brain" and vast microbiome, shapes mood and resilience, quietly influencing courage and calm. And the brain, ever the archivist, listens to these signals and turns them into memory and meaning.

---

* *The whisper of risk*: Intuition rarely arrives with certainty; it comes as a nudge, a quiet pull. Trusting it does not erase fear — it allows us to walk with it.

† *Coherence*: A scientific term for alignment of heart, brain, and nervous system rhythms. It is less about perfection, more about harmony in motion.

When the three play together, we enter a state of coherence — inner alignment that fosters clarity, resilience, and a sense of being deeply ourselves. It is not sameness but resonance, like a *raga*[*] tuned to the hour of dusk, or the layered polyphony[†] of voices rising in a cathedral — many notes, one harmony.

Of course, life is not always music. Some seasons bring clenched guts, racing hearts, restless minds. Stress scatters the orchestra, each part straining on its own. Yet even dissonance is a message: the body showing where tenderness is needed, where healing must return.

And always, after the noise, comes the invitation to breathe again, to begin again, to let the notes find their way back to each other.

I think of this when I remember meeting David — not just with my eyes, not just with my mind, but with the quiet compass of my whole being. My past had been filled with loves that flared and burned, dazzling but fleeting. With David, there was no lightning. His presence was like a steady note, a space to breathe more deeply. At first I mistook that stillness for lack of passion. Only later did I see it was the truest kind: patient, rooted, enduring.

Like every couple, we have weathered storms — especially raising Isabel, our radiant child whose rare condition reshaped our days in unexpected ways. Yet even in the hardest seasons, we have remained side by side. When the world grew messy and we lost our way, we learned to find each other again — sometimes in new places, sometimes in new ways. That rhythm of losing and returning has become its own comfort. I do not take it for granted. I know how easily such a love could have been missed if I had kept chasing only the spark and not the symphony.

---

* *Raga*: In Indian classical music, a raga is more than melody — it is tied to a time of day or season, summoning mood and memory. A reminder that harmony arises from attunement to the moment.

† *Polyphony*: In traditions from medieval cathedrals to Georgian choirs, polyphony layers independent voices into resonance. Coherence is not unison, but difference moving together.

Across cultures, the old stories remind us that the deepest knowing often lives beneath words — as surely as a *raga* carries memory in sound, or as polyphony weaves many voices into one breath. This is not superstition. It is the body's oldest wisdom: the wholeness of gut, heart, and brain when they move together like music.

So let your own orchestra swell. Trust that when the inner notes fall into tune, you are already home.

Tailwind

To live intuitively is not to reject thought.

It is to weave thought with feeling, memory with spirit.

It is to trust, in your bones, what is true for you, even when the map is blank, the room unfamiliar, and you stand alone in your knowing.

My intuition did not arrive as a gift, but as a response to life. From my earliest memory, I carried a sense of being slightly out of place. There was no single moment of abandonment, just the quiet discomfort that something about being me did not quite fit.

My father's presence was more longing than life, our bond stitched from scattered hours. My parents divorced before I turned seven, and the tapestry of my childhood was mostly woven by my mother's hands. She was caring, though rarely demonstrative, shaped by circumstance and the weight she carried alone.

So I ran outside beneath the tropical sun. I played tennis, drew, climbed trees, swam — throwing myself into sports and art, into any space where I could move, express, and breathe freely. In those places I found solace. Yet beyond the smiles, I sensed invisible boundaries. I was never quite a typical Malay girl, never quite a typical anything.

Even then, I understood — without language for it — that my difference was both a challenge and a dormant seed of power. The first flicker of intuition, urging me to seek belonging on my own terms.

Children who feel absence often learn to listen more keenly. I became fluent in the unspoken*, scanning rooms for safety in the shift of a face or the silence between words. That vigilance later grew into something else: the ability to read not just people, but possibility.

And yet, beneath the turbulence, a drive stirred. As if accomplishment might secure my place, I worked hard to shine. I painted weekly and once saw my work hang in the old National Art Gallery in Kuala Lumpur. I played gamelan and organ, collected medals on sports fields, debated on national stages, and later led teams. None of this was for display; it was instinct — a way of keeping the world kind by offering it my best.

Looking back, I see how hardship itself became my tailwind. What psychologists† now call growth after trauma was, for me, the alchemy of absence into resilience. Children who survive on subtle cues often turn them into the very skills that help them rise.

So much of my adult life has been a dance with this invitation. I left the safety of law when the world said it was foolish, and leapt into finance, then media. I moved to Germany for an international career, then began building companies of my own. At every turn, I followed the music of an inner knowing that whispered, *Go, even if you don't yet understand.*

Even now, I know writing is not a logical career path but an inevitable one. Every cell in me hums with resonance when words take shape on the page. Science calls it neuroplasticity‡; I call it the miracle of becoming new. Each leap lays new pathways between memory, reason, and imagination.

---

* *Limbic listening*: The brain's limbic system — tuned to emotion and belonging — grows sharper when children face absence, making them more sensitive to unspoken signals.

† *Growth after hardship*: Psychologists describe how adversity can spark unexpected strengths — resilience, meaning, empathy. Hardship can become tailwind.

‡ *Neuroplasticity*: The brain's lifelong ability to rewire itself, building new pathways whenever we step into the unknown. Each reinvention leaves the mind more flexible, more alive.

Over the years, I have learned to trust these signals the way I trust the sunrise. I notice when my chest tightens in a room, when an offer feels wrong, when a new friend feels instantly like kin, when a choice feels like destiny.

This is what I try to nurture in Camilla and Isabel: to honour the flicker in their hearts, the messages in their bellies, the strange knowing in their bones. Because to belong in the world, you must first belong to your own sensing.

As Hafiz wrote:

The small man builds cages for everyone he knows,
While the sage keeps dropping keys all night long,
For the beautiful, rowdy prisoners.

My intuition, born in the lonely gaps of childhood, has become my freedom. It is not escape but return — to wisdom within, to growth, to pivot, to becoming. To finding, again and again, my own home within.

Gamelan

Intuition was never a luxury in my life. It was daily bread, the invisible root beneath every journey, every choice, every becoming. To live intuitively is not to reject thinking, but to weave thought with feeling, memory with spirit. It is the inheritance of all who wish to live awake.

Intuition is not mystery, but the memory of wholeness — the knowing, somewhere deep within, of where you are meant to be.

I have always sensed this wisdom most clearly in music, especially in the ancient resonance of gamelan, whose echoes stretch across the Malay archipelago and beyond.

Gamelan is not only the music of palaces and sultans, though it has graced royal courts in Java, Bali, and Malaysia. It is also the heartbeat of villages, the pulse of weddings and harvests, the soundtrack of life shaped by rain, wind, and memory. Its bronze gongs, metallophones, xylophones, and drums have sounded for centuries, weaving communities from Sumatra to Lombok, from

Kelantan to Yogyakarta. From the Javanese *gamel*, meaning 'to strike,' the name itself carries the rhythm of its music.

But to play gamelan is more than striking an instrument. It is to listen and respond, to find your place in the living ensemble, and to offer your note only when the moment calls for it.

As a child, I sat at the centre of the orchestra, hands poised above the *bonang** — the golden kettle-gongs that thread the melodic line — where I felt the heartbeat of a tradition far older than myself.

Each piece of gamelan music carries intention: a beginning, a middle, an end. Its form is precise, built from cycles and interlocking melodies, rhythms that return and repeat with ancient patience. Yet within this structure, intuition breathes. The leader at the *bonang* reads the room, feels the energy, and makes subtle choices. The players adjust, anticipate, respond. The *bonang* does not dominate; it anchors and connects, guiding with steadiness — much like intuition itself, which carries us through the cycles of life with both structure and surrender.

I learned this early. At eleven, nervously leading the orchestra for the national television programme *Rasa Sayang*, hands on the *bonang*, I discovered the art of waiting for the right moment — to hold space, to sense when to lead and when to yield. That day, I understood what the elders meant: harmony comes from trust. Trust in tradition, trust in your fellow musicians, and trust in the inner knowing that lets the music carry you.

In gamelan, as in life, no single voice carries the whole story. We belong to something larger — a lineage, a land, a soundscape centuries old.

Every tradition whispers the same truth. Jewish mystics speak of the *bat kol*† — the daughter-voice that arrives as an echo. In

---

* *Bonang:* Sometimes called the "conductor without a baton." The bonang anchors the cycle, guiding shifts without dominating — a metaphor for intuition.

† *Bat Kol*: In Jewish mysticism, the *bat kol* ("daughter of a voice") is a soft divine echo that appears after prophecy — subtle, guiding, never thunderous.

Hindu thought, it is the *buddhi*[*] — the awakened intelligence beneath appearances. In Yoruba spirituality, the *ori inu*[†] — the wisdom within. Different names, same song: the quiet guidance that endures when reason falters.

Neuroscience now hums in harmony: the gut, the heart, even the skin — each an instrument in the body's orchestra of knowing. Ignore them, and life grows flat. Honour them, and you move whole, steady even through storm or change.

So when the world grows loud, or the map disappears, I remember the lesson of the gamelan. Let intuition be your *bonang* — listening, guiding, anchoring you through the unknown. Trust the wisdom that pulses beneath the noise, the root that holds you steady even as you change.

Intuition is not indulgence. It is inheritance: a deep current tying us to our ancestors, our communities, and our unfolding story.

May you move through life as the gamelan moves through a night of celebration: each note arising from listening, each silence full of meaning, every rhythm guiding you back to your home within.

---

* *Buddhi:* In Hindu philosophy, *buddhi* is the faculty of inner discernment — the clear intelligence that perceives truth beneath illusion.

† *Ori Inu:* In Yoruba spirituality, *ori inu* means "inner head" — the seat of wisdom and destiny, the part of us that knows our true path.

Chapter 13

The Point of No Return

One Way Journey

There is a moment in every journey when the wish to return becomes less a door and more a mirror. You stand at the threshold of home — the house that once held you, the language that shaped your first words, the people who remember the version of you that once fit easily in their hearts.

But the door no longer opens the way it used to. And the mirror no longer shows the face you once wore.

They say you can always go home. But the truth is, by the time you do, both you and "home" have changed. There is mourning in this realisation, a tenderness for the one who left believing return was always possible.

I did not leave under duress. There was no war, no tragedy. Malaysia was kind to me. As a Malay, I carried *Bumiputera** rights — a birthright designed to heal old wounds of colonisation, offering land, education, opportunity. It was an inheritance I did

* *Bumiputera:* Affirmative action policies in Malaysia granting Malays and indigenous groups preferential access to land, education, and business — a legacy of postcolonial repair.

not choose: a comfort that was also a question, gratitude braided with unease.

My country is young, restless, its skyline climbing like mushrooms after monsoon rain. For an ambitious Malay, the future gleams with possibility. And yet, I carried another hunger.

I remember playing with Wa beneath the *banyan** tree in our school compound, its roots tangled deep in the earth, its canopy sheltering our childhood secrets. Those afternoons still live in my body — warm, grounding, threaded with sweetness and sorrow. The tree reminds me that the old self, like the old house, cannot be lived into again.

Sometimes I walk through Kuala Lumpur and see the blaze of city lights, the skyline rising, but the map of who I might have been only flickers through the haze of memory. I honour the teenager who believed the door home would always stay open, even as I learn that some doors must remain closed, their stories carried instead in marrow.

When I return now, I am both guest and citizen. I slip between languages, stumble over old 1980s slang, reach for customs that no longer sit easily on me, like a childhood *baju kurung*† borrowed too late.

For years, I ached for home as destination. I thought laughter at a *mamak* stall or walking the old streets might restore me. But the self who belonged there cannot be re-inhabited. She lives within me still — in gestures, in Malay jokes, in scars — but she no longer waits at the threshold of a shell that has disappeared.

Becoming is a one-way journey. The road walked cannot be un-walked. There is grief in this, but relief too. I would not trade the woman I am now, not even for the ease of belonging written into my birthright.

Stamped Malay, many doors in Malaysia open for me. Univer-

* *Banyan:* Sacred across Asia, the banyan's aerial roots grow into groves, symbolising continuity and communal belonging.

† *Baju kurung* - Traditional Malay outfit.

sity places reserved, land to purchase, businesses supported. I would never have to prove my right to stay. My belonging there is unquestioned, written into law. And yet, I walked away.

I chose uncertainty. I stood in immigration offices with folders thick with evidence — degrees, contracts, bank statements, photographs — proving myself worthy to remain. I paid fees in British pounds and Euros, waited for verdicts, lived with the possibility of rejection.

Why step away from certainty? Because home was never only soil or law. I needed to feel who I was beyond inherited belonging, to discover who I might become when the ground beneath me was not guaranteed.

Even the great explorers knew this truth. Tenzing Norgay, born in a Himalayan village, returned a hero after summiting Everest with Edmund Hillary. *Khata,* scarves of blessing were draped across his shoulders, but he confessed later he felt caught between worlds. The boy who left was not the man who came back. The mountain had changed him.

I see my own reflection in his story. Like him, I carry deep love for the land that shaped me, and yet I am altered by the distances I have travelled. To grow is to climb a mountain that cannot be descended the same way.

There is no way back. Only forward.

So I honour the ache — the impossible wish to slip into my old *baju kurung* and find everything as it was. And I honour the relief of letting it go.

There is only the journey onward, carrying with me the scent of satay smoke, the sound of gamelan notes, the memory of my *baju kurung* worn with pride, and the golden anklet with a tiny bell, given by Wan Jah when I first learned to walk — a reminder to tether my heart, but never too tightly, to the place I once called home.

The Mirror of Comparison

I hold my longings the way I trace the lines on my own hand: familiar, shifting, always returning me to myself.

Why compare at all, you may ask? Because no matter how far we travel, we live in a world that prizes comparison. Everywhere there are scales and mile markers, subtle invitations to measure our worth against another's.

Our screens glow with other people's highlight reels — how quickly they built their lives, how effortlessly they seem to belong. It is tempting to shrink yourself to fit the mould, or rush to keep pace. But the way home was never meant to be a race.

The home within cannot be built on comparison. It can only be built on truth.

You are not late.

You are not behind.

Your belonging is not a borrowed costume.

The pull to compare is ancient. Our ancestors once read the faces around the fire to know if they were safe*. To be outcast meant danger; to stand apart was to risk hunger, or worse, loneliness. Comparison, then, is not vanity but an attempt to find our coordinates in a shifting world.

History has always carried this ache. In China, *miànzi* † — saving face — safeguarded reputation and survival. In India, caste etched comparison into work and marriage. In Greece, athletes were crowned while others were cast aside. Across cultures, comparison became both gate and wound: deciding who belonged, and who did not.

This inheritance reached me in smaller, more personal ways. My mother was caring, but attentive to social standing. When her

---

* *The fire's circle*: Anthropologists note that social exclusion once meant physical danger; neuroscience confirms rejection lights up the brain like pain. No wonder comparison still feels like survival.

† *Miànzi* (面子): In Chinese culture, "face" represents honour and standing; to lose face was to lose protection, to save it was to preserve belonging.

friends gathered for tea, the conversation often turned to whose daughter was studying abroad, whose son had married, whose family had achieved some new milestone. Every achievement became a kind of currency, exchanged across the table.

As a child, I shrank under it. My life felt constantly measured against someone else's yardstick. My success was a shadow of another's spotlight, my parents' reputation gently weighed in each conversation.

Decades later, comparison in Malaysia has only grown sharper. It is no longer only about education or wealth. Now it is how many times you have performed the pilgrimage to Mecca, how beautifully your children recite their Quranic verses, which handbag rests on your arm at a wedding. Social media only amplifies the chorus — every scroll a reminder of who seems richer, more accomplished, more pious.

Through it all, I find myself amused at my imperfections: not wearing *hijab*, chipped nail varnish on toes not suited for *wudu'*[*], often booking dinner tables in the narrow window between *Maghrib* and *Isya'*[†]. These small stumbles make me feel both in step and out of step — loyal to my people, yet slightly tilted in the group photo, the one with hair "free," always a little askew.

My friends and family, with affectionate laughter, remind me often: "We hope you will change, Nina." Their words are half-joke, half-very deep concern, carrying the fear for *jahannam*[‡] — invoked not as theology but as the shorthand of caution, of what happens if you wander too far.

I know this is not really about fault. It is about our human longing — to be seen as good, to be worthy, to belong to something larger than ourselves.

---

* *Hijab & wudu'*: Modesty in Islam is both faith and culture. *Wudu'*, the ritual washing before prayer, extends that sense of purity to the body itself.

† *Maghrib & Isya'*: Evening and night prayers, anchoring daily life in rhythm and remembrance, shaping even the social calendar.

‡ *Jahannam:* Qur'anic imagery of hell, often softened into humour in everyday talk, a reminder of how moral belonging is woven into cultural belonging.

The Courage for Self-Belonging

It is easy to feel worn down by the endless parade of "better."

Screens flash with other people's ease, their milestones, their belonging. Somewhere inside, a voice begins to whisper: not enough.

This ache is not only emotional. The brain feels comparison as threat. Old survival circuits flare; the same ones once tuned to the risk of being cast out from the fire. To be excluded was once to starve*. Today, it may only mean a scroll or a comment, but the body does not know the difference. It tightens, braces, waits.

And yet, the same body carries the way home. Self-compassion, gratitude, and mindful presence awaken gentler circuits — pathways of resilience and courage. Each time we return to our own values, our own breath, the brain rewires itself to feel safer in its own story.

Carl Jung called this individuation †: the lifelong task of becoming who you are, rather than a reflection of another's script. It asks us to see comparison for what it is. It is an old reflex, not the measure of our worth.

We can be proud of others and faithful to ourselves. We can thank our mothers for their hopes, even as we step gently in a different direction.

The home within cannot be built on comparison. It can only be built on truth.

You are not late.

You are not behind.

Your belonging is not a borrowed costume.

History offers companions on this path. Marina Abramović, raised behind borders in Belgrade, turned her own body into a

---

* Anthropologists remind us that exile once meant death; today, exclusion still registers in the body as pain. Belonging remains a primal need.

† *Individuation:* Carl Jung's term for the process of becoming your truest self, integrating both shadow and light.

canvas of courage. In *Rhythm 0*, she stood motionless for six hours as strangers were invited to use objects on her — from flowers to a loaded gun*. Some offered tenderness, others cruelty. She did not flinch. Her work revealed both the brutality and the beauty of human nature, showing that belonging sometimes requires us to stand unmasked, to risk everything, and to trust we will not break.

Nelson Mandela† carried another form of courage. Imprisoned for twenty-seven years, he emerged not with vengeance but with vision: reconciliation, a new belonging. His greatness was not fearlessness, but the choice to turn pain into a bridge wide enough for a nation.

Their lives remind us: courage is not the absence of fear, but the conversation between fear and hope. Each small act of bravery lays a new path within us, stone by stone.

My own story is less dramatic, but it carries the same thread. I have crossed borders, built new lives, spoken new languages. I have left safety for the hope of growth. Each time I shared my truth, even when it felt risky. I practiced courage. Each telling became a stone in the foundation of the home within me.

So let us be kind to ourselves in our longing to belong. Let us meet the part of us that aches for approval not with shame, but with compassion. Comparison will always beckon. But it is not the only path.

The home within is always a work in progress, built slowly, bravely, stone by stone, until we can stand, humble and whole, exactly where we are meant to be.

You are not late.

You are not lost.

You are already on your way home.

---

* *Abramović's lesson:* Her performances teach that presence itself — unmasked, unguarded — can be the deepest act of belonging.

† *Mandela's bridge:* His legacy shows that true courage often transforms private pain into public healing.

Not by Accident

Most of us are taught to avoid friction. To step around discomfort. To reach for the smoothest path.

We are told the best lives are seamless, swift, painless.

But that is not the soil in which true greatness grows.

If you look closely at those whose presence carries real strength, you will not see the absence of hardship. You will see the persistence of rising, again and again.

Think of Malala Yousafzai, whose voice was nearly silenced by violence yet returned stronger. Her courage rippling across continents*.

Think of Alaa Salah, the Sudanese student in white, standing tall above a sea of fear, singing† her people into courage and dignity.

The natural world teaches the same lesson.

The fern‡, ancient and enduring, has outlived extinctions, thriving wherever there is a crack of light.

The oak bends without breaking, its roots reaching deep for hidden waters.

The monarch butterfly§, fragile and luminous, flies across impossible distances on wings that have never known the path. Each storm shadows its journey, yet it endures. Resilience passed from one generation to the next.

True strength is not a fortress against the world, but a living dance with the winds that shape us. It is the willingness to bend, to root more deeply, to transform — even to break and begin again.

---

* Shot at 15 for defending girls' education, Malala survived and became the youngest-ever Nobel Peace Prize laureate — proof that harm can birth global hope.

† *Alaa Salah's chant:* Her image in white thobe and golden earrings became the symbol of Sudan's 2019 revolution, reminding us how a single voice can rally thousands.

‡ *Fern:* With a fossil record 360 million years old, the fern is living proof of patience — a green witness to extinctions and rebirths.

§ *Monarch butterfly:* Their migration spans up to 4,800 km, completed over several generations — each one flying a journey it has never taken before.

Strength is also the steadfast choice not to abandon the miracle of your own homecoming.

When we honour the fern's patience, the oak's endurance, and the monarch's fragile persistence, we remember: The ones who last are not those who avoid the storm, but those who allow it to make them new.

Strength is not an accident.

It is built in the slow, honourable act of rising after every fall, every failure, every moment you thought you had lost your way.

What if friction was not there to break us, but to sharpen us for the life ahead? Each stumble, each storm, each ache becomes part of the shaping. Never against us, but for us.

The ones who endures are not those who avoid the storm, but those who allow it to make them new.

Strength

Inna ma'al 'usri yusra — "With hardship comes ease."
- Al Quran 94:6

There comes a moment, sometimes as subtle as a sigh, sometimes as seismic as an earthquake, when you realise you cannot go back.

The door you left behind is no longer there.

The path has been swept clean by time and tears.

For me, the point of no return did not arrive in a single flash. It gathered year after year: through heartbreak and departure, through crossing borders and losing names, through becoming a mother, through starting, ending, and beginning again.

There was the marriage that ended. The new country where I felt both foreign and invisible. The diagnosis that altered my daughter's future and quietly rewrote my own.

Each time I searched for a way to undo, to return to what was, but it would not budge.

Slowly, I understood: life only moves forward.

What ancient wisdom calls rhythm, what the Qur'an promises as "with hardship comes ease,"* what every artist and athlete learns, was unfolding in me. I was being remade by friction. The old self could not be reclaimed, only honoured as foundation.

Over time, I saw that friction is not a curse but a teacher. Discomfort, grief, and repetition are chisels that shape us into something lasting. Sometimes the lesson comes as a breakdown. Sometimes as a breathless run. Sometimes as the steady act of refusing to quit. Grace hides in every setback.

Intention — *niyyah* — became my anchor, not only as a spiritual principle but as a way to harness the mind's capacity to change. Neuroscience shows that belief itself reshapes the brain. The difference between a fixed mindset ("I cannot change") and a growth mindset ("I can learn, I can adapt") is not just philosophy†; it is biology. Every intention, every conscious act of hope or effort, lays down a new pathway, a biological echo of desire.

And then there is courage. Not the absence of fear, but the willingness to risk oneself for what matters most. As the poet David Whyte‡ reminds us, courage is the measure of our participation in life, our choice to remain open even when certainty has gone.

When I trained for my first half-marathon in Berlin at forty-nine, I was not a runner§. My knees were untested, my lungs uncertain. Yet kilometre by kilometre, step by step, I learned to

* *Inna ma'al 'usri yusra* — "With hardship comes ease." Often recited for comfort, it affirms that struggle and relief are inseparable companions.

† *Growth mindset*: Psychologist Carol Dweck showed that seeing abilities as learnable fosters resilience and achievement. Neuroscience later confirmed this mindset reshapes neural pathways.

‡ *David Whyte on courage*: In *Consolations* (2014), he writes: "Courage is the measure of our heartfelt participation with life." For him, courage is not bravado, but presence.

§ Endurance sports often stand in for resilience. Anthropologists note that persistence running was once a survival trait; today, it mirrors the long arc of becoming — steady, imperfect, alive.

trust the slow miracle of persistence. The race was never about speed. It was about listening to the body, honouring intention, and moving forward anyway.

That finish line became a symbol: survival is not enough. It is endurance that teaches us to become.

Strength, I have learned, is built in the simple decision to keep walking — one belief, one intention, one trembling step at a time.

Keep walking home.

40-Love

As a girl growing up under the fierce equatorial sun, I was often reminded, sometimes with laughter, sometimes with concern, that no one would want to marry me because I was "too dark*, too unfeminine."

In 1980s Malaysia, marriage was not only a personal milestone but also a public achievement, a measure of whether a woman had been chosen, of whether she belonged. Aunties and neighbours did not mean harm, but their offhand comments carried weight. To be valued was to be seen as eligible.

It wasn't just family. On the school bus, in the classroom, boys teased me for being too bold, too much, too dark. Their words circled me like dragonflies, insistent and unkind. My skin did not fit the old story of beauty, another inheritance of colonial days, when lighter skin meant higher rank.

But I did not hide from the sun. I played tennis in the late afternoons, sweat salty on my lip, the courts radiating heat into my feet. At first, the racket felt heavy, but each swing rooted me more firmly in my own body.

---

* *Skin tone and colonial legacy*: In many Asian societies, colonial hierarchies reinforced older biases linking lighter skin with wealth and status. Outdoor labour was associated with poverty, while pale skin signified privilege. These values still influence beauty standards across Malaysia and beyond.

The world tried to tell me I was less. The sun never did. Its light reminded me that strength is not skin deep.

Often, tennis came before or after swimming lessons at the navy pool in Mindef, along Jalan Padang Tembak. There, under the open sky, water carried me. Swimming taught me rhythm: how to stretch and glide, when to kick, when to surface for breath. In the pool, I learned to float when I felt pulled under, to pause, to trust my body's return to the surface.

But it was tennis that became my teacher in resilience. Tennis is not won by a single spectacular shot but by the patient art of returning. You miss. You falter. The ball lands out, the net feels impossibly high, the angle wrong. You are seen in your mistakes. But the match is not over.

What matters is the next serve. Tennis rewards those who forgive themselves, who return to presence after failure. It is a sport of rhythm in repetition, not perfection*.

Under the sun and against the thump of the ball, I learned that resilience is not the story of never falling short. It is the decision to rise again, to let go of the last mistake, to meet the present moment with new determination.

Both tennis and swimming taught me that you cannot survive by wishing for different rules, different conditions, different skin.

You endure by learning rhythm: the timing of the breath, the patience of the return, the art of beginning again.

And so I began, slowly, to redefine beauty.

Not as the shade reflected in the mirror, nor the comments spoken behind my back, but as a deeper quality: forged in movement, in presence, in persistence.

No one told me that the most beautiful thing a girl can be is

---

* *Resilience as rhythm:* Research in psychology shows that resilience is less about avoiding mistakes and more about the willingness to recover, try again, and sustain rhythm. Athletes often describe this as "flow" — presence in the cycle of failure and return.

persistent. No one praised the courage it takes to return after failure, to keep showing up when the world says you are not enough.

But this is the lesson I carried:

that beauty is not a shade but a state of being.

It is the presence you bring to the court, the pool, the world. It is the promise you make to your own heart: that you will rise, again and again, no matter the score.

It took me years to believe this. I am still learning. But each return, whether in tennis or in life, reminds me that the real victory is not in never losing, but in coming back to yourself.

In tennis, there is a score called 40–Love*. It means you are one point away from victory. Yet the game is not over until you play that last point.

And so it is with us. The real victory is not perfection, but persistence, the willingness to begin again, to keep returning to yourself, no matter the score.

And when you find yourself on the losing side, remember:

the return is always yours to claim.

The Call of the Sea

As a child in Malaysia, my world was edged by water: rivers winding through villages, waterfalls tumbling in green forests, islands scattered like jewels along the coast, and the South China Sea breathing at the country's edge.

Our meals were a daily testimony to the sea's generosity. White rice, a flash of green from *kangkung* or *pucuk ubi*†, and always fish, squid, or prawns — fresh from the market or gifted by a neighbour. To serve seafood was not luxury but rhythm, so ordi-

---

* *40–Love*: In tennis scoring, "love" means zero, thought to come from the French *l'œuf* (egg), symbolising nothing. "40–Love" means the server is one point away from winning the game.

† *Kangkung* and *pucuk ubi*: Simple village greens that embody Southeast Asian kitchens, reminders that belonging is often found in the most ordinary meals.

nary it felt eternal, as if the ocean's abundance would always be waiting at the door.

Even then, I sensed that the tide never returned in quite the same way. The fish on our table changed with the seasons, or appeared in new recipes as the monsoon came and went. The meals evolved, subtly but inevitably.

Change, I learned, was constant — gentle or wild, never pausing to ask permission.

Years later, drifting weightless among the reefs on my first dive in Boracay island, I finally saw what the kitchen table had only hinted at: the sea is a living metaphor for transformation.

Corals are architects of renewal. After storms shatter a reef or bleaching leaves it ghost-pale, coral does not cling to its old form. If even a single polyp survives, rebuilding begins: slow, persistent, layer upon layer, until a new reef rises*. Not a replica, but something altered, carrying memory into possibility. Broken fragments drift in the current, seeking new ground, carrying the past into the hope of the new.

The reef is never what it was, and yet it is beautiful — perhaps more so for the evidence of its survival.

Mangroves †, abundant in Malaysia too, are sculptors of change. They root themselves in shifting tides, living half in water and half on land, never belonging fully to either. Their tangled roots weave the soil together, making new ground where once there was only mud and salt. When storms tear at their branches, mangroves bend. From broken limbs, new shoots rise. Their seeds float on currents, carried to distant shores, where they begin new forests far from home. Mangroves cradle entire communities — human and wild — offering shelter, protection, and new beginnings.

---

* *Coral recruitment*: A scientific phrase for how even fragments can seed new life, a metaphor for resilience after rupture.

† *Mangroves*: Trees that live between worlds, showing how thresholds can be fertile ground rather than fracture.

The younger version of me did not know I was already practicing this kind of change: learning to adapt with every meal, every shifting season, every goodbye.

The sea never truly returns to what it was, and neither do we. Each phase, each loss, each storm — external or within — moves us further from what was familiar, and further into who we are becoming.

We are called, like coral and mangrove, to let go of the idea of return. There is no going back, only going forward: sometimes with scars, sometimes with gifts, always with change as our companion.

You do not have to live by the sea to know this truth. The city, the desert, the mountain — each has its own tides of becoming. Wherever you are, life will pull you forward. Circumstance, grief, joy, or discovery will make it impossible to remain unchanged.

You can cling to the old shoreline, or you can learn from the sea: to build from what remains, to root in shifting ground, to create new beauty from loss, to be carried by the current into a future you cannot fully imagine.

If you find yourself longing for what is gone, aching for a home you can no longer enter, remember the sea's lesson:

You do not need to return as who you were. You are here to renew, to repair, to begin again.

Whether at the family table or alone in the deep blue water, the art is not in resisting change, but in letting it shape you into someone new. Someone stronger, more tender, more alive.

The sea teaches us that return is not a circle but a spiral.

Every arrival is a beginning.

Every loss is a seed.

And each of us, wherever we are, carries the salt and memory of the places we have loved. We build our own reef, our own mangrove forest, our own home within.

The sea calls all of us to become, never just returning, always becoming.

Grow Slow

Not all growth arrives with a bang.

Some transformations begin softly: the patient ascent of a cycad*, the slow unfurling of a fern in the tropical forest, the poised stillness of a hand in yoga's *mudra*†, signalling readiness even in silence.

The world is noisy with urgencies: fast results, instant arrivals, the loud performance of strength. But nature's oldest teachers move to another rhythm.

When David and I celebrated our marriage at the Palm House at Hortus Botanicus in Amsterdam, one of the oldest botanical gardens in Europe, we wanted our promise to be witnessed by ancient cycads. These "living fossils" have endured for more than 280 million years, surviving empires, ice ages, even the dinosaurs. Their growth is almost invisible, only a handful of new fronds each year, yet they persist for centuries, sometimes millennia. Among them, love felt not fleeting but enduring. Their presence reminded us that true strength is born of patience and persistence.

Resilience, in both nature and human history, does not come from avoiding devastation, but from beginning again after it.

This is the law of the slow:

Wholeness is not speed.

Wholeness is an architecture, built stone by stone, intention by intention.

All that is strong in you is shaped not by what happens quickly, but by what unfolds over time — the patient work of rising after each fall, of adapting rather than resisting.

After Isabel's diagnosis, I turned to yoga for daily comfort. In yoga, the simple turn of a hand into a *mudra* is a gesture of pres-

---

* *Cycads:* Living fossils that predate flowers and fruit. Some are older than entire civilisations, reminding us that endurance is its own form of beauty.

† *Mudra:* A gesture that directs energy. A reminder that transformation often begins not in sweeping change, but in the smallest shift of intention.

ence and intention. Even in stillness, a *mudra* embodies the truth that change can begin with the smallest, most deliberate movement.

Science now echoes this wisdom*: slow, mindful movement calms the nervous system, lowers the heart rate, and restores clarity. A reset of ancient biology, a return to the wisdom of being.

The wisdom of slow is honoured across cultures. Lao Tzu reminds us: "Nature does not hurry, yet everything is accomplished." The Japanese practice of kaizen trusts in steady improvement through small steps. Even Einstein credited patience, not brilliance, for his discoveries.

With every slow season, a new facet of yourself is revealed, if you dare to trust that the patient work of becoming is its own kind of prayer.

The world will always say it is better to be fast than whole. But true becoming is not about speed. It is surrender to process, the steady unfolding of your life, each time a little more yourself.

There is magic in what grows slowly, like the cycad, unfurling strength one frond at a time, enduring what others cannot imagine.

So too within you: let your heart hold that posture — steady, persistent, unhurried — and you will find yourself enduring and renewing, becoming more yourself with every slow season.

This is the miracle of truly living:
to grow,
to love,
to promise,
not in haste but with the patience of roots,
and the grace of ancient witnesses.
In a world that rushes, allow yourself to grow slow.

* *The science of slow:* Practices like yoga and tai chi soothe the nervous system, showing that patience is not only poetic but physiological.

Amor Fati

The point of no return is not a tragedy. For those who live across borders and cultures, it may sometimes feel that way. But it is a sacred crossing, a threshold every soul is called to meet.

You cannot go back.

You cannot shrink to fit the story you have outgrown, nor unravel the spiral of growth already begun.

I must confess: there are nights when I look up at the northern sky, resting in the vastness between stars, and I wonder — should I have returned home to Malaysia, anchoring myself in the sweet ache of old belonging?

Should I have taken that job in Singapore, closer to my parents, closer to a culture that honours the tending of aging parents?

Would it have been wiser to offer my mother, despite our emotional distance, the nearness of a daughter, instead of living as an island held by chosen friends?

These are the questions that haunt many who have crossed borders and lived through seismic change.

The "what ifs" trail behind us like shadows. At times, I feel the dull ache of the life not chosen. But even regret can become a kind of compass, pointing me onward. Psychologists call this counterfactual thinking*: the mind's way of tracing roads not taken, not only to torment us but to teach. Left unchecked, it keeps us circling the past. Welcomed with compassion, it returns us to the blessing of now.

The Stoics called this *amor fati*, to love one's fate†. To let every twist of the story, even regret, become a companion on the road to becoming. Perhaps the greatest kindness is this: to greet each

---

* *Counterfactual thinking*: The mind's habit of imagining alternate paths, which can sting with regret but also point toward meaning and new choices.

† *Amor fati*: The Stoic invitation to embrace fate in its entirety — joy, loss, and uncertainty alike — as necessary to becoming.

"what if" with tenderness, to listen, then to bless it and let it rest — returning, again and again, to the unfinished beauty of what is.

When Isabel's diagnosis arrived like a sudden storm, I asked myself: was it wise to have another child at forty-one? Did my optimism tip fate's scales? I know, by every scientific measure, that her rare mutation was not caused by my age or David's. Yet grief circled still, searching for maps back to the life that could have been.

Narrative therapy* reminds us: we are never just the sum of our "what ifs." We can re-author our stories, weaving meaning from uncertainty. The butterfly cannot crawl back into the chrysalis. The acorn cannot return to seed. You cannot unlearn the lessons or unlove the people who have remade you.

Even the cosmos tells this story. Galaxies are born of collapse, clouds of dust and gas falling inward to ignite new stars. Supernovas scatter elements that seed planets, and eventually, life itself. Our very bodies carry traces of those ancient stars. Science calls it cosmic dust†. Faith reminds us that there is breath and mercy behind it.

Like *ikebana*‡, where heaven, earth, and humanity are placed in delicate balance, we too are bridges between soil and sky.

The cosmos never returns to what it was. It expands, transforms, carries memory in every particle of light. So do we. Each decision, heartbreak, and hesitation alters us. You cannot return to who you were, but you can expand into who you are becoming.

Even as the universe expands, so does the human heart.

It learns to hold more: sorrow, joy, and all the selves you have ever been.

---

* *Narrative therapy:* A practice that helps us reframe our life stories, shifting from regret to agency.

† *Star-stuff:* The carbon, oxygen, and iron in our bodies were forged in ancient stars. We are literally made of the cosmos.

‡ *Ikebana:* The Japanese art of arranging flowers in balance between heaven, earth, and humanity. It reminds us that beauty often lives in asymmetry, space, and what is left unsaid.

Your story is not a closed circle but a widening spiral.

You can always return to yourself, not to the person you once were, but to the truest room within — the place that holds your longing, your regret, your hope, your courage, your becoming.

I build this home within, brick of truth by brick. Play the *Hari Raya* song. Cook rice the way Wan Jah once did. Let rituals of memory be the gravity that steadies my orbit.

This is the invitation: to live at your own pace, to trust your orbit, to meet friction with patience and courage. When the world shouts for speed, choose presence. When comparison whispers smallness, remember the vastness of your becoming — like a galaxy, always expanding.

When "what if" visits, greet it kindly. Let it teach, then let it rest. Life is not built from what is lost, but from what remains — from the joy still unwritten.

This is *amor fati*: to love not only the story you have lived, but also the unanswered questions. To trust that the path you walk now is enough.

If you find yourself standing at the edge of your own sacred crossing, remember: you are not meant to go back. You are made to gather all you have been and step forward into the next spiral of your orbit.

The home within is not a fixed place, but the unrepeatable map of your journey — the courage to keep becoming, to shine in your own corner of the sky.

You are not lacking.

You are not broken.

Threshold Wisdoms

There is a moment at the edge of every becoming when you are called to pause. Not to rush into what waits beyond, but to linger in the stillness where old stories are laid to rest.

The point of no return is not always a leap.

Sometimes it is a lingering, a sacred in-breath before the next exhale.

In that stillness, the ache of change begins to turn into wisdom. You become both witness and architect of your unfolding.

I remember the day I left my childhood home for boarding school, suitcase heavy with sadness more than clothes. My mother's face at the gate, her voice steady as she handed me into a new world: "You are going to be OK."

That first night, and many after, the air felt cold and strange. I hated almost everything about boarding school: the regimented days, the sameness of routine, the constant surveillance, the taste of watered-down curry with sweet-water fish that carried absence more than nourishment.

And yet, it was this separation, this discipline, this loneliness, that carved in me the part determined to dream beyond what I was handed. Boarding school taught me my first lessons in how to live among strangers, how to obey rules without losing myself, how to survive in the crowd without vanishing. If I had never disliked it so deeply, perhaps I would never have longed so fiercely to fly, to build a life of my own, to discover where I belong.

We all carry these thresholds: the first steps away, the farewells to parents, to childhood friendships, to forgotten versions of ourselves. The girl who played gamelan. The girl who played tennis beneath the tropical sun. The young artist who did not yet know she would never paint in the same way again.

Some goodbyes are sharp and sudden. Others hide in the slow loosening of expectation, the silent grief of outgrowing comforts that once felt like shelter.

Anthropologists call this liminality: the sacred in-between where the old self falls away and the new has not yet formed*.

Across cultures, thresholds are honoured with ritual. The

---

* *Liminality:* Anthropologist Arnold van Gennep described the in-between phase of rites of passage — no longer who you were, not yet who you are becoming.

Maasai leap over fire as a sign of crossing*. In Malay tradition, families gather for a majlis *doa selamat*, prayers spoken over turmeric rice, blessing the unknown together†.

History, too, is full of thresholds: migrations that reshaped nations, the first footprints on the moon, the fall of the Berlin Wall, the long shadow of the COVID pandemic. Each moment marked by pause, release, and the courage to step into the unfamiliar.

The poet John O'Donohue wrote: "A threshold is not a simple boundary; it is a frontier that divides two different territories, rhythms, and atmospheres."‡ To cross is to accept you will never be the same.

Often, it is the arrival, not the leaving, that feels heaviest. Every step toward newness trembles with the weight of meaning.

At thresholds, your fiercest teachers appear. Sometimes it is the world that rejects you. Sometimes it is your own restless longing. Sometimes it is the wound that asks you to hide.

I have met them too: in sleepless, tearful nights, in decisions that asked for more courage than I thought I had, in moments when I was both storm and shelter, fighting for my own freedom.

Science reminds us that the brain resists change, even good change§. The discomfort is not failure, but the mind quietly rewiring itself, making space for a new way of living.

And what you refuse to learn will circle back, wearing new faces, until you are ready to greet it — not as punishment, but as blessing.

---

* *Maasai fire leap:* A rite of passage marking courage and the crossing into adulthood.

† *Majlis doa selamat:* A Malay gathering for prayer and blessing, often with turmeric rice, before a new journey or transition.

‡ *John O'Donohue:* Irish poet-philosopher whose writings framed thresholds as sacred frontiers of transformation.

§ *Neuroplasticity:* When we face change, the brain first triggers fear responses; with repetition, it forges new pathways that allow adaptation and growth.

Chapter 14

Me in The World

Who Are You?

There comes a turning after every long journey. Not at a border or on a plane, but somewhere inward.

It is the place you reach when the ache for return softens, when the storm of becoming recedes, and what rises instead is gentler: the longing to reach for others, not from hunger, but from a place of fullness.

For years I thought belonging meant arrival: a postcode, a seat at the table, a story that stayed put. I believed love required sacrifice, that to be accepted I must bend, merge, even disappear. I measured my worth by the weather of others, over-giving and over-bending, afraid that without the "we" I would not survive.

Without thinking, my voice adapted to every room. My accent shifted, my laughter stretched or softened, my language bent to fit* . I became a culture chameleon, at ease with the aristocrat and the

* *Code-switching*: A term from sociolinguistics describing how bilingual or bicultural people adjust language and behaviour depending on context. It has long been a survival skill for migrants navigating many worlds.

banana seller alike, colouring myself to match the rhythm of the room.

Looking back, I see it was both art and armour. I belonged everywhere, and yet, for many years, nowhere. Friends who met me in one setting and saw me in another sometimes wondered: Who is the real Nina? At times, I envied those whose sense of self did not flex with every new room.

It is a bittersweet love — to want so deeply to meet others where they are, to carry tenderness for many, and yet to ache for one place where you are seen as whole. That ache, I know now, was also the soil of my compassion.

Life, in its mercy, sent me another blessing: when you begin to live from your own frequency, not just as a chameleon but as your truest self, the world has a way of sending you those rare souls who recognise your essence no matter the shape you take. Regina, my podcasting mentor, who sees me beyond the surface. Bart and Henk, my helpful neighbours in de Jordaan, whose kindness feels like brotherly home itself. They remind me there are people who sense your spirit before they judge your accent, who see the thread of your heart regardless of the hues you wear*.

These kinships are not magic, but resonance — the invisible frequency that calls to those meant to find you*. And when you meet them, you know: recognition, softness, the grace of being held as you are.

Sometimes, if you are very fortunate, one such soul arrives — a friendship so steadfast it feels marked by fate, travelling with you across countries and seasons, through laughter and heartbreak alike. I have been gifted such a companion, and his story I will share soon.

And so I have learned: some of us are not meant to root in place, but in practice.

---

* *Resonance:* Social psychology suggests that deep connection often arises not from similarity but from the felt sense of recognition — when someone perceives your essence beyond appearances.

Not in permanent arrival, but in the spiralling rhythm of return.

True belonging is not perfect adaptation, but presence.

It is not shrinking in the "we," but showing up with empathy while keeping the courage to remain distinct.

Now I carry the gift of adaptation with gratitude — as echo of ancestors, as tribute to resilience — but I no longer confuse it with erasure. I no longer believe I must shape-shift to be loved.

Instead, I build ground in ritual, in presence, in the daily architecture within. Belonging is not found in perfect fitting-in, but in the steady return to myself: wherever I am, however I sound, with whomever I sit at the table.

Sometimes, with morning tea in hand, I still notice the old reflex to perform. And then I return. I sit in the gentle weight of who I am, in all my languages and shades, knowing now that I am enough.

If you too have ever felt like a chameleon, may you find your own ritual of return — a way to remember that you are enough, wherever you land, and that the world is always conspiring to send you those who will see your light, in every form it takes.

Everyone Needs a 'Fred'

"Friendship is unnecessary, like philosophy, like art...
It has no survival value; rather it is one of those things that give value to survival."
— C.S. Lewis*

We all need at least one friendship that is more than company, more than convenience. A bond that reminds us we are already at home in ourselves.

---

* *C.S. Lewis:* In *The Four Loves* (1960), Lewis describes friendship as unnecessary for survival but essential for meaning — like art or philosophy, not needed to live, but needed to live well.

If life is a search for belonging, sometimes the universe gifts us a kindred spirit whose presence steadies us in ways no place or achievement ever could.

I was lucky enough to find such a friend.

Ours has always been platonic, steady, generous, never shadowed by confusion. We laughed through heartbreaks, carried each other through missteps, and celebrated small victories with genuine delight. What made it endure was never grand declarations, but the simple grace of caring without measure, of cheering without envy.

We met in Germany, long before marriages and children. I was older, already wandering. He was barely twenty, still becoming. Yet somehow our spirits arrived in the same season. Since then, our lives have crossed through Berlin bunkers, Paris attics, Amsterdam kitchens, and countless tables where friendship proved itself stronger than distance or time.

He played with Camilla when she was small, brought Isabel a giant bear years later, and along the way witnessed me in all my selves: reckless and responsible, grieving and joyous, mother and wife. I have seen him move from youth into marriage, into fatherhood, into wisdom. Our roots have wound quietly beneath the surfaces of our separate lives, entwined by trust and humility.

Philosophers call this the highest kind of friendship, the one rooted not in utility or pleasure but in virtue, where two souls delight in each other's growth*. Modern science echoes them: deep friendship calms the body, strengthens the heart, builds resilience. Presence itself becomes medicine†.

Sometimes the greatest sanctuary is not a place but a person.

---

* Aristotle: In *Nicomachean Ethics*, he distinguishes between friendships of utility, pleasure, and virtue — the highest being grounded in mutual goodness and growth.

† *Harvard Study of Adult Development:* This 80-year study found that close friendships are among the strongest predictors of well-being and longevity, often more than wealth or fame.

A companion with whom you need not compete, perform, or shrink. Where your essence is met with gratitude.

Some friendships are not measured by geography or years, but by the certainty they leave in your bones: that you are, and have always been, at home.

And if you are still searching, may you remember: the universe is always quietly conspiring to bring us not just to the places where we belong, but to the people whose hearts are waiting to welcome us exactly as we are.

If you have ever lost friends, or feared you are too different to belong, trust this: the universe is not done surprising you. It only takes one soul who sees you as you are to change the course of your journey. And when that person arrives, may you have the courage to recognise them, and the grace to be that kind of friend in return.

Be yourself.

Trust that your people will find you.

(*For Frederic, with gratitude, la Lutte*)

Light and Shadow

For much of my life, I try to read the room, so I can soften my edges for comfort's sake.

In Malaysia, I learned early that goodness meant blending in. *"Jangan conteng arang di muka mak ayah,"** I was told: never bring shame to the family. My actions were not mine alone; every choice reflected on my parents, my siblings, the entire clan. Reputation was shared currency. Even at the table, kindness meant leaving the last piece of *kuih*† for someone else. Belonging shel-

* *Jangan conteng arang di muka mak ayah*: A Malay proverb meaning "do not smear charcoal on your parents' face." It reflects the deep tie between individual behaviour and family honour.

† *Kuih*: Traditional Malay sweets or cakes, often served at gatherings. Leaving the last piece for someone else embodies courtesy and self-restraint.

tered us, but it also asked us to disappear a little for the sake of harmony.

At boarding school, I met another form of belonging — spiritual, protective at times, punishing at others. Prayers five times daily were mandatory. To miss one was not just my lapse but the community's. Seniors, the *kakak usrah*[*], sometimes guided with warmth, sometimes with fear. Once, I was even asked to prove I had my period to excuse a missed prayer. A small humiliation, but one that stayed with me: the reminder that even faith could be policed, privacy surrendered in the name of unity.

Later, in the Netherlands, I stepped into the opposite script. Individuality was prized. You spoke your mind, sent a *tikkie*[†] for the coffee you covered, said no without guilt. Children learned to debate, not defer. It was liberating, and sometimes lonely. Community was optional, not given. Yet here too, warmth had its place: the Dutch cherish *gezelligheid*[‡] — that untranslatable comfort of gathering, the wide table where everyone belongs.

So I have come to see that every culture carries both light and shadow. In Malaysia, collectivism could shelter or suffocate. In the Netherlands, individuality could free or isolate. Both knew, in their own ways, how to hold the tribe when it mattered[§].

Now I see these tensions everywhere. My daughter and her friends call out fakeness online, finding community in naming struggles rather than hiding them. Whether in Kuala Lumpur or Amsterdam, authenticity has become its own virtue. Perhaps the

---

* *Kakak usrah*: Literally "Islamic study-circle sisters." In Malaysian Muslim schools, *usrah* are small religious study groups led by seniors, sometimes nurturing, sometimes strict.

† *Tikkie* — A Dutch mobile payment app that lets friends instantly settle small shared costs, like coffee or groceries. More than technology, it reflects the Dutch ethos of fairness and clarity in social life: every person carries their share, no awkwardness left at the table.

‡ *Gezelligheid*: A Dutch word with no direct English equivalent, describing the warmth of togetherness, often around food or shared space.

§ Threshold of cultures: Across the world, societies negotiate between the pull of "we" (collective) and "me" (individual). Each contains both shelter and shadow.

pendulum is seeking a new rhythm, a table where "we" and "me" can sit together without fear.

I have stumbled on both sides: shrinking to fit, bending until I broke, insisting on authenticity at the cost of tenderness. Each experience has become a stone in the foundation of my becoming.

Forgiveness — slow, imperfect, ongoing — is the ground I stand on now. Forgiveness for those who policed me, for those who misunderstood me. Forgiveness for myself, too, for the bending, the breaking, the mistakes along the way.

Acceptance has followed. The past is unchangeable, its lessons written into me whether I asked for them or not. I do not need to carry every burden, nor erase every gift. I can honour what was, and with love, choose what to keep and what to lay down.

So I offer my weathered self as a gift: daughter and ancestor, questioner and survivor, Malaysian and not, Dutch and not.

If you too feel pulled between the "we" of heritage and the "me" of becoming, you are not alone. This is the spiral we are all living now. Perhaps, in this meeting of worlds, you are building a new home — one where the fullness of who you are is not only allowed, but needed.

Real belonging is found where authenticity and connection meet. May the future be a long table where both "we" and "me" can eat together, side by side, unafraid.

Don't Sweat the Small Stuff

How do we root ourselves — not in a postcode or a plan, but in the living present — when our lives are shaped by movement and change?

For those who cross borders or weather upheaval, belonging is not a destination. It is a practice, a gentle craft: drawing new maps from presence, not permanence.

Small rituals — what some call micro-anchors* — tether us when everything else shifts. The morning cup of tea, a breath before a meal, the pause to say thank you. Each repetition tells the body: you are here, you are safe, you are not lost.

Ancient traditions have always known this. The tea ceremony in Japan. The call to prayer rising and falling five times a day in Islam. The Benedictine rhythm of *ora et labora*†, pray and work. The Malay courtesy of leaving the last piece of *kuih*‡ untouched. Rituals do not give us permanence. They give us presence. They remind us that meaning lives not only in milestones, but in the gentle repetition of care.

For me, sweat became such a ritual.

I found it most powerfully in a *Bikram*§ yoga studio on Sarphatistraat in Amsterdam, years ago, as my marriage was unraveling. In that forty-degree room, nothing outside could intrude. My only task was to stand in the mirror, breathe, and move through the same twenty-six postures. The heat drew heaviness from my bones. The sweat on my skin felt like release, each droplet a quiet shedding of what no longer served me.

I learned there that resilience is not always triumph. Sometimes it is simply the decision to return: breath after breath, pose after pose, day after day.

Of course, there are days the rituals slip away. I forget, I rush,

---

* *Micro-anchors* — Psychologists use this term for small, repeated rituals that ground the nervous system. A daily tea, prayer, or breath acts as a signal of safety, building resilience.

† *Ora et labora* — Latin for "pray and work," the guiding motto of St. Benedict's monastic rule. It shaped centuries of monastic life by weaving rhythm and balance into the ordinary.

‡ *Kuih* — Malay cakes or sweets, often shared at gatherings. Courtesy is shown by leaving the last piece for someone else, a quiet gesture of restraint and generosity.

§ *Bikram yoga* — A style of hot yoga with 26 fixed postures, practiced in heated rooms. Controversial in origin, yet for many practitioners the heat and repetition became a crucible of release and resilience.

life interrupts. But missing a day is not failure. What matters is the gentle return. To begin again, without punishment or regret.

And you do not need yoga to find this. Your anchor might be an evening walk, the kneading of bread dough, the light across your kitchen floor, a private prayer, or singing along to your daughter's favourite Taylor Swift song. The form does not matter. The returning does.

Habit is not only comfort. It is resilience. It steadies us the way lotus roots hold fast in mud while the flowers open above water.

Presence is your soil. Ritual your stem. Together they carry you upward, no matter how the waters shift.

Home is wherever you let yourself fully arrive.

When walking, walk.

When eating, eat.

When sweating, sweat.

And above all, do not sweat the small stuff.

When living, live.

A Gift to Yourself

Before I could build a new life, I had to forgive the old one.

This meant, above all, softening my resentment toward my parents. Not to erase the hard parts of childhood, but to see the whole, complicated picture with gentler eyes.

Mine was a childhood of independence and achievement — music, sports, art prizes, the applause that came from being excellent in public. I learned how to shine. But when others speak of cozy laps or soft-voiced tenderness, I remember instead the absence of that particular love.

A few years after my parents' marriage dissolved in eighties Malaysia that still stigmatised the word divorce, my brother Dzul and I were sent to boarding schools. We were the only children from a broken home, pitied and observed, always a little outside the circle. My father was a distant constellation, adding new chapters that rarely included us. Home became synonymous with longing, sweetness tinged with absence.

And yet, within that absence, seeds of resilience began to take root. I became resourceful, determined, hungry to prove myself in every room. What was missing gave me both my ache and my drive.

For years, I pressed forward, filling the silence with achievements. But in my twenties, living alone in England, the ache surfaced at last — like hunger I could not name.

Forgiveness began with seeing my parents as human. My mother, carrying her own pain, doing what she could in a society that judged her for being a divorcee. My father, chasing meaning in all the wrong places, never realising what he might have built simply by staying close. They, too, carried wounds I could not see.

Anger, I have learned, has its place. It signals that something mattered. But it cannot hold the whole story. To forgive was to let the past breathe without tightening my fist.

And of course, I have caused hurt too — reckless words, naïve mistakes, choices made in confusion. Forgiving myself has been just as hard. Self-compassion, as Dr. Kristin Neff* reminds us, is offering ourselves the same kindness we would give a dear friend. Each act of self-forgiveness interrupts shame and makes space for hope.

Forgiveness is not a single moment, but a season. Sometimes a trickle, sometimes a downpour. At first impossible, and then, one day, the ground feels softer. There is space for something new to grow.

Forgiveness is also compost†: the slow, unseen work of turning what was broken into the very soil from which new life can rise.

It is never only private. Forgiveness shapes what we pass on.

---

* *Kristin Neff* — Psychologist and pioneer of self-compassion research. She describes self-forgiveness as offering ourselves the same kindness we would extend to a friend.

† *Compost* — In ecology, decay becomes fertile soil. As metaphor, it speaks to transformation: pain and failure turned into nutrients for growth.

In my auntie's house on my grandparents' land, the ancestral portraits look down, silent witnesses to old wounds. I see how easily sorrow could become inheritance.

To forgive is to say: it stops here. My children will not pay for my parents' pain.

We are all babushka dolls*, carrying those who came before us, but also the power to change the ending.

Forgiveness is choice — an inborn superpower. It is how we open windows in a house shut too long. Not to absolve or forget, but to let the wind move through, to breathe the world as it is: imperfect, unfinished, but real.

So if you carry anger or regret, know you are not alone. This is the universal task of being human.

Here is your invitation:

soften your grip.

Begin again.

Forgiveness is not a gift to the past, but to your own becoming. And every act of self-compassion is a blueprint for belonging — within yourself, and for all who come after.

Crossings

To live between worlds is to become, almost inevitably, a builder of bridges.

Airports, WhatsApp groups, kitchens — these are my crossing points, the improvised architecture of connection. I've learned to reach across, to create belonging even as everything shifts beneath my feet.

Consider the Golden Gate † in San Francisco, once called

* *Babushka dolls* — Russian nesting dolls, used as symbols of generational inheritance. They remind us that we carry layers of ancestry and memory, but also the possibility of shaping a new story.

† *Golden Gate Bridge* — Completed in 1937, once deemed "impossible." At the time, it was the longest suspension bridge in the world, quickly becoming a global symbol of perseverance.

impossible, then raised against all odds in 1937. More than steel and cables, it became proof that even the widest waters can be spanned by vision and persistence.

Amsterdam, my home now, is stitched together by a thousand bridges*, each one a quiet reminder that marsh can be made into city, chaos into community.

Not every bridge, though, is forever. Some, like the Mostar Bridge† in Bosnia, fell to war and were later rebuilt as monuments of healing. Others, like London Bridge, were dismantled and carried elsewhere, transformed into new meaning. Some collapse, reminding us that loss can be the first step toward renewal.

In our own lives too, not every crossing endures. I think of the Malaysian women I once gathered with abroad, weaving east and west around tables of *nasi lemak*‡. We laughed about politics, teased about our *Mat Salleh*§ husbands, slipped "*lah*" into every sentence, and found comfort in food and rhythm. But kinship is never only joy. It carries rivalry, comparison, or quiet estrangement. A WhatsApp group can feel like a lifeline one year, then fall silent the next.

Even the sturdiest bridge cannot withstand every storm.

Bridges are not homes. They are places of passage, letting life flow through.

Sometimes we are the bridge, steady beneath the weight of others. Sometimes we are the traveller, tentative yet grateful for

---

* *Amsterdam's bridges* — The city has more than 1,200 bridges, many dating to the 17th century. They turned wetlands into a thriving city of canals, earning Amsterdam its nickname, "Venice of the North."

† *Mostar Bridge* — Built by the Ottomans in the 16th century, destroyed in 1993 during the Bosnian War, and rebuilt in 2004 as a UNESCO World Heritage Site. Today it stands as a symbol of reconciliation.

‡ *Nasi lemak* — Often called Malaysia's national dish: rice cooked in coconut milk and pandan, with sambal, anchovies, peanuts, and egg. It is both meal and metaphor for home.

§ *Mat Salleh* — A colloquial Malaysian term for white Westerners. Its origins are debated, but in everyday speech it carries playful, sometimes teasing tones, reflecting Malaysia's colonial past and cultural mixing.

safe crossing. At times we are the river, carrying stories, reshaping what lies beneath. Or the fog, softening edges, reminding us that not every path is meant to be clear.

I have carried others through difficult seasons, only to watch them move on without looking back. That, too, is grace. The reward is not in being remembered, but in knowing you made the crossing possible.

Connection, I have learned, is less about permanence and more about presence. The Sufis call it "two mirrors facing each other" — a meeting of souls where recognition alone is enough.

Friendship at its best is tending the bridge when you can, knowing the river will still rise and fall. Sometimes the bridge endures; sometimes it collapses. To love is to accept this impermanence, not as failure but as life.

If you find yourself mourning a connection that has passed, know this: you are not failing. You are being human.

True connection does not dissolve you; it deepens you. We are all, at different times, the bridge, the traveller, the water, the fog. Each role necessary. Each crossing sacred.

So build, repair, release. Offer your whole self. Trust that what is meant to stay will stay, and what is meant to pass will find its own way.

Flow

There is a threshold at the heart of every journey, the quiet pause after a crossing, the breath before the next hello. It is here that self-acceptance becomes sanctuary — not resignation, but a living welcome to your unfinished self.

Our minds are quick to find fault. Psychologists call this the negativity bias*: our brains catch the bad like Velcro, while the good slips away like Teflon.

---

* *Negativity bias* — Evolution shaped us to notice threats more than blessings, ensuring survival but also making self-critique louder than self-kindness.

For years, I was fluent in self-critique, replaying regrets as if they were proof of who I was. When Isabel's neurological condition appeared, grief hollowed me. Night after night, I lay awake combing through memories, searching for the sign I missed, the mistake I must have made. I blamed myself even for what I could never have known.

And it was not only the big things. Friction with family or friends often sent me spiralling inward, convinced that every misunderstanding must be my fault. Many of us carry this habit — the belief that if we could just get it all right, everything would stay whole.

But healing has its own voice.

Every act of self-compassion whispers to the body: you are safe, even here, even now.

Philosophy offers the same reminder. The Greeks called it metanoia*, the capacity to turn and change. Zen speaks of *shoshin*†, beginner's mind — the practice of meeting each moment as new.

My own life has been stitched with mistakes: lost keys, spilled coffee, mismatched shoes, WhatsApp exits followed by sheepish returns. Once, I even told a Dutch shopkeeper I loved their kisses instead of their cushions‡.

Yet the older I get, the more I see that life is just this: missteps and recoveries, stitched together by forgiveness and the choice to keep showing up.

Mistakes are not detours; they are the staircase itself. Neuroscience confirms what the heart already knows: every thought,

---

* *Metanoia* — A Greek term meaning "change of mind" or turning toward a truer path, often used in philosophy and spirituality.

† *Shoshin* (初心) — In Zen Buddhism, "beginner's mind," approaching each moment with openness and curiosity, even for the experienced.

‡ *Kussen/kus mix-up* — In Dutch, *kussen* means "cushions" but also "kisses" (plural). A common source of comic misunderstandings for learners.

every act, every error changes the brain, shaping us as we go*. To accept mistakes is not defeat. It is proof of being alive.

Living globally sharpens this truth. You become a collector of accents and airport rituals, a connoisseur of where to find instant noodles in any city. Home is not always four walls. Sometimes it is laughing at your own dark humour across time zones, a cup of morning tea, the memory of familiar faces flickering on your screen.

Acceptance, I have learned, is welcoming the whole, untidy self: the one who doubts, the one who dares, the one who gets lost, the one who starts again. The more room I make for my unfinishedness, the more room I have for the world — its surprising kindness, its unexpected joys, its tender reversals.

Life itself has a sense of humour.

It is an endless open house: doors creaking, guests arriving, the occasional odd sock under the couch. Even the mess has its own hospitality.

You do not have to choose between selfhood and togetherness. You can love with the doors of your heart wide open — not to be emptied, but to welcome those who honour the architecture of your soul. Integration, as Dr. Daniel Siegel† describes it, is this weaving of scattered parts into wholeness.

Love flourishes in spaciousness, not perfection. You have earned your right to belong to yourself. From that fullness, you can belong with others — not from lack, but from overflow.

Let presence be your new address.

And if you are waiting to "arrive," to be perfect or complete, remember: there is more beauty in becoming than in being finished. The guesthouse of your heart is always open — unfinished, yet enough.

---

* *Norman Doidge* — Psychiatrist whose work on neuroplasticity showed that the brain continually reshapes itself through experience.

† *Integration* — Psychiatrist Daniel Siegel's idea that wholeness comes from linking together different parts of ourselves, creating resilience and joy.

So bless the mess. Laugh at the detours. Paint your doors *grachten gordel groen**, the green of Amsterdam's canal belt, a reminder that even here, in this city of bridges and tides, I can build sanctuary.

The Malay proverb says: *Rumah siap, pahat masih berbunyi.* The house is finished, but the hammering continues. So does the home within you.

---

* *Grachten gordel groen* — The deep green paint used on doors and shutters in Amsterdam's canal district. Protected as part of the UNESCO heritage, it symbolises continuity, identity, and place.

Chapter 15

The Return Home

Spiral Homecoming

There is a moment in every journey when the search softens. The longing to arrive dissolves, not because we have found the perfect place, but because we have learned to carry a resting place within ourselves.

The spiral* teaches us this: we do not return as we left. Every crossing — each heartbreak, each joy, each small act of survival — reshapes us. The journey does not trace a circle but turns inward, ever deeper, carrying us closer to the self who has held all our versions.

To spiral back is never to repeat. A circle closes, but a spiral expands. Each return brings us to the same place, yet never the same self: wider or narrower, softer or stronger, but always changed. In this way, life is less about arriving at a final point and more about deepening into layers of understanding. The spiral is

* The spiral is one of nature's most recurring patterns. The Fibonacci sequence — 1, 1, 2, 3, 5, 8... — creates a spiral that appears in seashells, sunflowers, hurricanes, and galaxies. Philosophers and mystics have long seen in it a symbol of growth, expansion, and the infinite.

the geometry of growth — not erasing what was, but enfolding it into what is still to come.

Home was never a postcode.

It is the work of gathering: the girl who left, the mother who stayed, the friend who welcomed, the wanderer who endured. Nothing is wasted. Each part belongs.

I remember her still: the little girl with the pencil case with the red London double-decker bus, sketching her place into being. Long before that, in the garden of our home in Malaysia, she would crouch low to watch centipedes curl into spirals at the lightest touch of a stick*. She did not know then that her search would become her compass, that her ache would one day become her gift.

The spiral is written everywhere — in galaxies, seashells, storms, even in the double helix of our DNA†. Our very code of life is spiral, a reminder that becoming is inscribed in us from the beginning.

So may you carry this with you: every leaving is also a beginning. Every return is a deeper becoming. The spiral is wide enough to hold it all — and so are you.

And perhaps, like the centipede in the garden, we, too, are called to curl inward for a time — not to hide, but to remember that within the smallest coil, the whole journey is already waiting.

---

* In Polynesian cultures (e.g. Samoan), centipedes appear in tattoo symbolism as protectors. The symbol *fa'atualoa*, such as in Marquesan designs, embodies long life, vigilance, and warding off harm. Some folklore elsewhere holds centipedes as guardians against evil or misfortune, though these beliefs are less consistently documented.

† The double helix DNA first described by James Watson and Francis Crick in *Nature* (1953) — is a spiral staircase of paired molecules. This structure, confirmed by Rosalind Franklin's X-ray diffraction images, revealed that the very code of life carries the form of a spiral. It is both literal and symbolic proof that continuity and transformation are inscribed in us from the beginning.

Gathering the Selves

If you could step inside the architecture of your own heart, what would you find?

For me, it is a mosaic: the little girl with the red pencil pouch, the anxious young woman in airports, the mother who grieved the language her daughters did not inherit, the leader, the entrepreneur, the lover, the friend, the pilgrim. Each one lives here still, held in gentle containment by my aging brown skin and by the rituals that have carried me across worlds.

Some days bring sweetness — a warm *karipap*[*] gifted by my friend Amie, or sipping the last drop of BOH tea from the Cameron Highlands on a winter afternoon. Other days, the sharpness of parting rises again: the ache of a farewell left unsaid, the persistent tang of longing for a place I cannot quite name.

We spend so much of our lives believing wholeness is something to win or earn, always waiting for us elsewhere. But wholeness, the sages remind us, is not an arrival. It is gathering: turning toward every version of ourselves and saying,

Come in. You belong.

Neuroscience now echoes what Sufis and sages long knew: the self is never finished, but always being woven. The mind does not erase what wounds us; it folds them in, shaping new meaning from old pain. Psychology reminds us that becoming is not about perfection, but about gathering our scattered pieces—the proud and the fragile, the sweet and the bitter, the bold and the uncertain—and offering them all a place at the long table.

Eastern philosophy describes wholeness as harmony, not flawlessness. Lao Tzu wrote, *"At the center of your being you have the answer; you know who you are and you know what you want."*[†]

---

[*] *Karipap* — A small, crescent-shaped pastry filled with spiced potatoes, meat, or sardines. A beloved Malaysian snack, often shared at tea time or family gatherings.

[†] Lao Tzu, *Tao Te Ching* (c. 4th century BCE). A foundational Taoist text emphasising harmony, balance, and living in accordance with the Tao (the Way).

Taoism teaches that *yin and yang* are not opposites but companions: every sweetness contains its shadow, every loss its hidden gift.

Sufi wisdom says the heart is a guesthouse, each visitor a teacher. Rumi urged us to greet even sorrow as a companion with something to reveal. The old Malay saying, *air dicincang takkan putus* — water that's been cut will always flow together again — reminds us that what separates in one moment may return quietly in another.*

And if I close my eyes, I can taste every version of myself: the sweet gula Melaka† of joy, the bitterness of regret, the salt of tears, the still resilience that endured every crossing.

So I gather my selves: the ones who tried too hard, the ones who loved beyond language, the ones who were judged and rejected, the ones who learned to let go. Each is offered a place at the long table, not because they were always wise, but because they are all part of my becoming. They remain as permanent guests in the long ancestral home.

This is integration—not the effort to force myself into wholeness, but the gentler act of allowing the sweet and the bitter, the old and the new, to coexist. It is the miracle of becoming the place you have been seeking, not through striving, but through welcome.

A home within, shaped by the gentle rhythm of return. *Seperti sirih pulang ke gagang*‡ — the old Malay proverb: like the betel leaf returning to its stem, we find our way back — not just to a place, but to the source within.

What parts of you are still waiting for your invitation home?

---

* Malay proverb: *air dicincang takkan putus* — Used to describe family ties and the inevitability of reunion despite quarrels or separation.

† *Gula Melaka* — A rich, smoky palm sugar made from the sap of coconut or *nipa* palms, widely used in Malaysian desserts like *cendol* and *kuih*. It evokes nostalgia and home for many in the Malay archipelago.

‡ Malay proverb: *seperti sirih pulang ke gagang* — A metaphor for returning to origins, home, or rightful belonging.

To gather the selves is to spiral back through memory, not to stay in the past, but to welcome each part into the home within.

Stones That Remember

At the edge of the Atlantic, I stand before the Dolmen des Trois Pierres in Saint-Nazaire, a 6,000-year-old tomb of stacked granite* . The stones remind me that we are all guests here, tracing the same questions that shaped lives long before ours. What does it mean to belong? To endure? To leave a mark, not of conquest, but of care?

These ancient monoliths show that humans have always reached for meaning in the face of movement. Long before passports or property lines, we raised stones to say: we were here, we belonged, we mattered.

Memory, too, is like stone. Neuroscience tells us it is not a fixed archive but a living network, reshaped each time we recall. Our senses lay down markers: the sound of rain on a zinc roof, curry leaves sizzling in hot oil, the cadence of "Mind the gap!" on the London tube, the bells of the Westerkerk, the tear of baguette crust in a French boulangerie. Our bodies remember where love and safety once lived — sometimes more deeply than the mind can name†.

Psychology calls these "ancestral echoes": gestures, rituals, griefs passed down through generations. In Malay, we call it *ilmu turun-temurun*‡ — wisdom that travels in how we greet the morning, share food, or a prayer for the living and the dead.

---

* Dolmens are Neolithic stone tombs, built 5,000–7,000 years ago across Europe and Asia. They are among humanity's earliest monuments, often aligned with the sun, moon, or stars, marking burial sites and communal rituals of belonging and remembrance.

† Each act of recall reshapes neural pathways, blending past and present (Daniel L. Schacter, *The Seven Sins of Memory*, 2001).

‡ *Ilmu turun-temurun* — A Malay phrase meaning "knowledge handed down," referring to inherited wisdom passed through daily practices, gestures, and oral tradition.

In these moments of stillness, I feel all the places I have lived converging. The damp mornings of Raub, the golden haze of Loire vineyards, the drizzle of London, the grim winters of Gütersloh, the canals of Amsterdam. My skin still holds Kuala Lumpur's humidity; my laughter the sweetness of *teh tarik*; my resilience the sharpness of German frost. I have learned to savour *les petits plaisirs* — the ripe *Reine Claude* plum, the extra hour in a random bookshop in London.

The stones of Loire-Atlantique do not ask us to forget. They hold space for everything we carry. *Orang berbudi kita berbahasa, orang memberi kita merasa* — those who show kindness, we honour with grace; those who offer, we receive with gratitude. The Malay heart is built on reciprocity, just as the French spirit is built on reverence for land and tradition.

To belong is not about settling or wandering, but about presence. These stones did not try to escape time; they entered it fully. They remind me that belonging is not possession but honour, not conquest but care.

Perhaps this is what longing asks of us: to become like the stones themselves, both witnesses and guests, listening to the ground and leaving behind something true and tender.

Belonging, too, is a spiral. Each place we live becomes another stone on the path, not a circle of return but a deepening. Spirals appear in seashells, in storms over oceans, in galaxies across the night sky, in Celtic carvings, in Malay batik, in sacred mandalas. They carry the same truth: each return brings us back, but never as the same self. We come altered, always becoming.

The stones remind us that to belong is not only to arrive, but to keep walking the spiral of memory and presence. To honour the ground. To offer care. To carry forward what each place has given, trusting that every step leaves behind not conquest but tenderness.

Home as Rhythm

What is home, if not the rhythm you return to when the world grows quiet?

I find it in the smallest rituals: rooibos tea in the evening, the slow grace of kneading dough when homesickness lingers, the scent of something baking warming my old Jordaanse huis. It is also there in the gentle walk after dinner through Amsterdam's canals, bicycles gliding past, the glow of windows in winter, the *clic-clac* of footsteps on redbrick streets. Wandering, returning, each sound carries me quietly back to myself.

At other times, home takes the shape of rhythm: the *planta-tacón* of flamenco shoes striking the wooden floor of a Sevilla studio in 2004, the heel and sole echoing in sharp, fierce cadence. Walking, moving, letting energy build through streets or dance has always been how I return to my heart, especially when belonging feels far away.

Philosophers remind us that home is not a fixed place, but a return to what is essential. Heidegger spoke of dwelling as the act of *verweilen bei den Dingen* — to linger with what is here, to let ourselves truly belong to the people and places that shape us*.

Psychology tells us belonging grows in repetition — in rituals that soothe the nervous system and signal safety. Neuroscience confirms it: the body craves rhythm. Even a simple walk regulates the mind, calms anxiety, and knits memory and creativity back together. Running or dancing can become meditation, a way for body and mind to braid themselves whole.

I think of my solo pilgrimage: a 67-kilometre walk during the Covid lockdown of 2021, from my house in Amsterdam to my small country house in Venhuizen. Three days of walking, alone beneath the wide Dutch sky, undisturbed by planes and accompanied only by wind. Each step became a prayer, a conversation

* Heidegger, *Building Dwelling Thinking* (1951): dwelling is not simply inhabiting, but "to linger" in relation to things, people, and place.

with every self I had ever been. By the end, I realised that belonging is not always in the destination, but in the steady return of breath and footfall, a way of piecing the world back together street by street, memory by memory, until home emerges, not as a place but as a rhythm in the bones.

History and art whisper the same truth: every culture has painted, sung, or walked its way back to belonging. In Japanese *karesansui** gardens, monks rake stones into rippling patterns as daily meditation. Indigenous Australians sing songlines† across the land, mapping geography and spirit. Renaissance painters filled canvases with golden light spilling from windows and tables, reminders of gathering and return.

From the East, Tagore‡ reminds, "Let your life lightly dance on the edges of time like dew on the tip of a leaf."

Sometimes I imagine them in conversation: Heidegger urging us to linger with what is real, Tagore inviting us to dance lightly with what is fleeting. Together, they remind me that home is found not in arrival, but in the courage to return again and again, and in the tenderness with which we greet each moment.

For me, home is no longer a location.

It is a practice of connection.

It is the permission to set down the suitcase, to stop auditioning, to breathe fully into my bones.

It is the art of coming back to myself, again and again, with every crossing, with every loss, with every gentle step, with every *bonang* beat on the earth.

Even after heartbreak, and especially then, home is the rhythm that waits, steady as the tide. Perhaps this is the truest belonging of all: not a place, but a rhythm that moves through us, carrying us back, again and again, to the home within.

---

* *Karesansui* — Japanese dry landscape or "Zen gardens," where raked sand and stones symbolise rippling water and invite contemplation.

† Indigenous Australian "songlines" are oral maps sung across landscapes, embedding geography, law, and spirituality into memory and tradition.

‡ Rabindranath Tagore, *Collected Poems and Plays* (1912).

The Benediction of Self-Belonging

"Indeed, with hardship comes ease." (Qur'an 94:6)

If you are reading this, searching for one place to call home, let this be your reminder: you are already carrying it within you.

You are the only constant, the ground beneath your own feet. All the places you have loved, the languages you have borrowed, the selves you have been — they live here, in the tender architecture of your belonging.

The way forward is not certainty but courage. Not perfection but love.

Let pain, fear, and even the unwanted chapters be not detours, but threads in your becoming. The home within is made whole not by avoidance, but by welcome. And when the next door opens, may you have the courage to walk into rooms you do not yet recognise, to greet strangers with tenderness, to wander the face of the earth with wonder. Taste what is unfamiliar. Ask what was once forbidden.

The Japanese speak of *omotenashi* — the art of giving without transaction, of offering one's presence as gift. May you practice it not only with others, but with yourself. To meet your own heart with generosity, without condition. To belong, not because you have earned it, but because you are here.

The poet Mary Oliver, who found holiness in the ordinary — in geese flying low, in wildflowers opening unnoticed, in the hush of morning walks — once asked: *"What is it you plan to do with your one wild and precious life?"*

Let your answer be this: to belong fully, to love without measure, to gather your scattered selves into the home within.

Selamat pulang. Welcome home.

This has always been your home within.

Gifts for The Journey

These words are not instructions,
but lanterns to light your own journey, wherever it may lead.

To Camilla, My Wildflower

My Camilla,

You arrived with fierce eyes and a spirit that would not be tamed. From the start I have known you were never mine to shape. I am here to guide, to witness, to love—and then to let you go, wings whole.

This is not a map. It is a lantern. Take what helps, leave what doesn't. You are building something entirely your own.

The world will be loud with rules and expectations. When it gets noisy, keep this small truth in your chest: you do not have to fit. You only need to root. When others do not understand you, go inward. That is where your real home is anchored.

These pages are offerings—tools for your backpack, spices for your kitchen. The recipe belongs to you. Make it unfamiliar if you must. Make it yours.

Love your sister fiercely, but never at the cost of your own edges. Do not trade your boldness for someone else's ease. She is a gift to you; you are a gift to yourself.

Hardness will come. When it does, remember this: standing is not the only way to survive. Sometimes you must fly. Sometimes you must land and breathe. Always be brave enough to begin again.

I have tried to give you wings and roots, freedom and foundation, curiosity and a compass. My deepest hope is that you feel safe enough to question what I have given you and brave enough to choose what is yours.

Your life will not and should not mirror mine. New rituals, new joys, new definitions are not disloyalty; they are legacy.

I will always be a home you can return to. But you are your own country now. I love who you are today, and I cannot wait to meet who you become.

Love,
Mama

Letter to Isabel, My Guru

My Isabel,

Before you arrived I thought I knew the shape of love. Then you came and taught me another grammar altogether — softer, slower, wider than I had imagined possible.

You do not speak in sentences the world easily reads. You have taught me to listen without translating, to receive gestures as whole truths. That unspoken language has taught me more about tenderness than a thousand words ever could.

You have stretched my patience into a kind of grace I did not know I held. My days learned new rhythms because of you. Your routine has anchored me; your needs have made me brave in ways I had not been before.

You have shown me how to sit in uncertainty without rushing to fix it. Where the world wants answers, you have taught me the dignity of waiting, the quiet courage of being present. When everything else was loud and urgent, you taught me to find peace in not knowing and to discover joy in the smallest, most unexpected moments — a sunbeam on the floor, the blink of a bird, the way your laugh lifts a room.

If the world ever tries to measure you by its narrow rules, know this: you are not behind. You are not less. You are everything your spirit was meant to be. Your difference is not a deficit; it is a kind of luminous map. You are, in every way, enough.

You are a teacher as much as you are my child. You show me how to love without agenda, how to notice without judgment, how to celebrate the small, precarious miracles of daily life. Your life is not a shadow; it is a constellation.

I am honoured, more than words can hold, that your soul chose this road with me. I will walk beside you always: to steady, to laugh, to hold, to learn. Mostly, to love.

Always,
Mama

The Wanderer's Manifesto

Place your hand on your heart. Remember: you are alive not only in joy, but also in doubt, in ache, in becoming.

You have crossed continents, languages, and invisible borders within. You have carried heartbreak and hope in the same breath. And still, you rise.

You are not here to stay unchanged. Every crossing, every loss, every beginning has shaped you.

You belong not because of a postcode, but because you claim yourself.

You are allowed to question.

You are allowed to outgrow.

You are allowed to root and to fly.

Home is not behind you. It is not waiting ahead. It lives inside you — expanding with every step.

Let your story be witness. Let it be light. Tell it so others know they are not alone. You are not here to perform. You are not waiting for permission. You are worthy, exactly as you are.

This is what courage looks like.

This is what persistence feels like.

This is how we build shelter again and again: in honesty, in story, in each other.

May you be kind to yourself. May you walk boldly.

May your heart draw its own map.

This is the return.

This is the home within.

May you always find your way home.

Vale in Luce - Farewell in light.

Gratitude Without Borders

This is not just my story. It is ours.

No journey is ever walked alone. This book, like my life, has been held together by the hands, hearts, and voices of those who carried me when I could not carry myself, who lifted me when I faltered, and who reminded me that I was never truly lost.

To my family: you are the root and the rhythm beneath every page. Mama, Ayah, and Dzul, you are the soil of my becoming. David, Camilla, and Isabel, you are my heartbeats — the truest measure of home.

To the big-hearted friends who wove me into kinship wherever I landed, whether your names appear in these chapters or not, thank you for your love, patience, laughter, and faith. Every call, every meal, every embrace across oceans is etched into these pages. You are part of my constellation*. If your name is not written, know it is only because my gratitude is too abundant for ink to hold.

To Kak Nad, who gifted me the Foreword, to Mimi and early readers who lent your voices in praise and endorsement: your solidarity has strengthened this work.

To colleagues, kind strangers, and the ancestors whose wisdom guided me: know that you too are carried here. This book exists because of a constellation of love, friendship, and faith. You are my living proof that belonging is never solitary, but a shared and sacred architecture of home. Thank you. *Terima kasih.*

---

* Page 157 — Chapter 10: *Nothing is ours except time.*

Notes & Inspirations

This book was written with the companionship of many voices across time: scientists, poets, philosophers, mystics, and storytellers whose words helped me find language for the ache and wonder of becoming.

Their works did not simply inform the writing. They accompanied me like friends around a table, reminding me that becoming is never a solitary act, but a chorus of ancient and modern, intimate and universal, stitched themselves into this book. May their echoes also keep you company, as you walk your own path of becoming.

Faith and Ancestral wisdom,

I carried the Qur'an's promise in *Surah Al-Inshirah — with hardship comes ease.* Malay proverbs echoed through my bones: *seperti sirih pulang ke gagang* (like the betel leaf returning to its stem). My grandmother Wan Jah's gift of reading dreams and signs in nature was another compass, reminding me that intuition is inheritance. So too were the traditions of Africa, Celtic lands, Māori elders, Jewish mystics, and Native Americans, each affirming that guidance is carried in bloodlines and in bones.

Neuroscience

I leaned on Stephen Porges' *Polyvagal Theory*, Daniel Siegel's *Mindsight*, and Julianne Holt-Lunstad's research on the link between connection and longevity. Nicholas Christakis and James Fowler's *Connected* reminded me that our social circles ripple through us, often unseen but always shaping who we become.

Psychology and philosophy

I held Brené Brown's invitation to vulnerability in *Daring Greatly*, Jung's vision of individuation, and Seneca's quiet reminders that becoming has always been a human concern. Jim Rohn's observation that we are shaped by the five people closest to us, stayed close as I reflected on friendship and chosen family.

Eastern Wisdom

I returned to the *Tao Te Ching* and Lao Tzu's assurance that wholeness comes not through striving but allowing. Rumi whispered through these pages, urging me to "seek those who fan your flames." The Hermetic laws of rhythm and polarity confirmed what my Malay heart already knew: with hardship comes ease.

Zen Philosophy

I learned again that presence is home. A single unhurried cup of tea, a raked garden, a fleeting moment of stillness — each is enough. Wabi-sabi showed me that cracks are not flaws but invitations for light. And *ichi-go ichi-e* — one time, one meeting — shaped how I hold the preciousness of friendship and belonging.

Western Philosophy

I carried Aristotle's vision of friendship as "a single soul dwelling in two bodies." The Stoics, especially Marcus Aurelius and Epictetus, reminded me that resilience lives in clarity and discipline. The existentialists – Kierkegaard, Nietzsche, Camus – echoed through my reflections on freedom and meaning, while Simone de Beauvoir's insistence that we create ourselves through action shaped how I understood identity, especially as a woman moving across worlds.

Arts & Literature

Marina Abramović's *Rhythm 0* and *The Artist is Present*, and Frida Kahlo's paintings and journals, revealed the courage it takes to be truly seen. Wassily Kandinsky, Georgia O'Keeffe, and Miles Davis gave me a language of intuition – through colour, shape, and sound. C. S. Lewis, in *The Four Loves*, reminded me of the sacred ordinariness of friendship, while Anaïs Nin's words on blossoming guided my reflections on motherhood.

History

I found kinship in Tenzing Norgay's reflections after Everest: a reminder that once you climb into another version of yourself, return is never simple.

Modern Voices

I carried Oprah Winfrey's trust in intuition and Steve Jobs' reminder that "you can only connect the dots looking backward." Both offered courage to follow whispers into the unknown.